It's true that James is a freak—he works harder, is more dedicated, exudes enthusiasm, always puts ethics first, and makes millions of dollars as both a broker and investor. But—good news—James has detailed every move you should make if you want to mimic his achievements. This book is a step-by-step guide to your journey to top performance . . . if not freakdom.

—Blaine Strickland
bestselling author and coach

The Insider's Edge to Real Estate Investing is fantastic! James breaks down the intricate and complex terms for the beginner investor in easy digestible bites! If you are thinking about investing in real estate, this book should become your Bible!

—Beth Azor
Founder and owner of Azor Advisory Services

THE INSIDER'S EDGE TO REAL ESTATE INVESTING

GAME-CHANGING STRATEGIES TO OUTPERFORM THE MARKET

JAMES P. NELSON WITH **RACHEL HARTMAN**

New York Chicago San Francisco Athens London Madrid
Mexico City Milan New Delhi Singapore Sydney Toronto

In memory of Jim Kinsey, who had the insider's edge in real estate and life because he understood that success and happiness are about having great relationships built on trust. I was gifted the chance to have Jim as a dear friend and partner in Avison Young's Tri-State Investment Sales Group. Moreover, he was my sounding board for more than 20 years. He passed away unexpectedly in 2021, but his wisdom lives on in those he knew during his time with us.

Regardless of how busy he was, Jim always had time for mentoring up-and-coming investors and for his family. His achievements both at work and at home have served as examples I strive to follow each day. A portion of the book's proceeds will be sent to the Bowery Mission, which he supported. My personal tribute to him can be found at rew-online.com/a-tribute-to-jim-kinsey/.

Thank you, Jim, for the role model you were to me and for giving back to so many along the way.

1 2 3 4 5 6 7 8 9   LCR   28 27 26 25 24 23

ISBN   978-1-264-86599-4
MHID   1-264-86599-6

e-ISBN   978-1-264-86673-1
e-MHID   1-264-86673-9

This publication is designed to provide accurate and authoritative information in regard to the subject matter covered. It is sold with the understanding that neither the author nor the publisher is engaged in rendering legal, accounting, securities trading, or other professional services. If legal advice or other expert assistance is required, the services of a competent professional person should be sought.
> —*From a Declaration of Principles Jointly Adopted by a Committee of the American Bar Association and a Committee of Publishers and Associations*

Library of Congress Cataloging-in-Publication Data

Names: Nelson, James (Writer on real estate investing), author.
Title: The insider's edge to real estate investing : game-changing strategies to outperform the market / James Nelson.
Description: New York : McGraw Hill Education, 2023. | Includes bibliographical references and index. | Summary: "Up your game in today's lucrative real estate market with 10 proven steps from investing insider James Nelson"— Provided by publisher.
Identifiers: LCCN 2022057312 (print) | LCCN 2022057313 (ebook) | ISBN 9781264865994 (hardback) | ISBN 9781264866731 (ebook)
Subjects: LCSH: Real estate investment. | Finance, Personal. | Investments.
Classification: LCC HD1382.5 .N45 2023 (print) | LCC HD1382.5 (ebook) | DDC 332.63/24—dc23/eng/20221202
LC record available at https://lccn.loc.gov/2022057312
LC ebook record available at https://lccn.loc.gov/2022057313

McGraw Hill books are available at special quantity discounts to use as premiums and sales promotions or for use in corporate training programs. To contact a representative, please visit the Contact Us pages at www.mhprofessional.com.

McGraw Hill is committed to making our products accessible to all learners. To learn more about the available support and accommodations we offer, please contact us at accessibility@mheducation.com. We also participate in the Access Text Network (www.accesstext.org), and ATN members may submit requests through ATN.

CONTENTS

FOREWORD
by Ryan Serhant

As a broker in New York City, I get asked for advice all the time. I'm always happy to share my knowledge about the industry with one big exception. When clients of mine come to me and say, "Ryan, renting out our apartment worked out so well. We want to up our game! We're thinking about buying a building. What do we do and how do we get started? What do we need to know about investing in commercial real estate to be successful?" My response is simple and always the same. Call James Nelson! He's the best! As one of the top investment sale brokers in New York City who has closed hundreds of deals, his experience and expertise can't be matched. James knows the ins and outs of every step of the process, from finding the right property and the right tenants to raising capital. As a broker I know how complicated a real estate transaction can get, but James's approach to investing is straightforward, clear, and best of all, it works.

There is *no one* more perfectly positioned to write this book than James. *The Insider's Edge to Real Estate Investing* is a gift to anyone who is thinking about investing in real estate because it tells you *exactly* what to do. Think of this book as a blueprint for getting ahead in the real estate game. *The Insider's Edge to Real Estate Investing* covers all the bases . . . from the fundamentals of investing to putting together the right team of people. Investing in real estate is a big decision, but after reading this book you will be ready to *take action*. You can move forward knowing you've armed yourself with the knowledge you need to be a successful buyer. What are you waiting for? Start reading! Dive into this book, soak up all of James's unique wisdom, and get ready to reap successes.

PROLOGUE

Growing up, nobody in my family invested in—or even dabbled in—real estate, with one exception: my grandfather. Even he wasn't strictly a full-time investor; by day, he worked in the auto industry. Over the years, he successfully ran multiple car dealerships. On the side, he invested in properties to create returns and build his retirement savings.

As a child and later in college, I observed my grandfather's real estate investment portfolio grow. While I didn't fully understand it back then, his investments typically consisted of buying the land for his auto dealerships and then leasing that property back to his business. His taste for real estate investments didn't end there; he also bought and sold homes. It wasn't unusual for him to have his hands in multiple projects at once: fixing up places, renting them out, putting them on the market, and so on.

Throughout the time I knew him, my grandfather prioritized real estate over other types of investments. He shied away from the stock market, perhaps because he felt like an outsider in that space. In real estate, however, he was a true insider. He possessed a deep understanding of properties, returns, and his own personal tolerance for risk. Thus, he chose to keep his savings—and earnings—in that market. I recall hearing him often repeat the adage first coined by Mark Twain, "Buy land, they're not making any more of it."[1]

My grandfather had an innate appreciation for assets that could hold their value—and better yet, grow in their worth, especially when they did so because of his work. He knew when to acquire properties, how to reposition them, and how to structure deals for a great return. Perhaps most importantly, he wasn't afraid to dive in and take calculated risks. Sure, he learned from his mistakes, and then applied those lessons to his next efforts. His drive for discovering new insights and moving forward reflected in the real estate empire he built over the course of his lifetime.

Only after I had graduated from college did I begin to fully grasp my grandfather's dealings. Reflecting on it now, I am forever grateful for that glimpse into the strategies he incorporated. It certainly played a role in my life later, when I ended up walking the streets of New York with a job in real estate.

My pathway to the financial capital of the world and a career in real estate wasn't direct. I was born in Madison, Wisconsin, where my father worked as a general practitioner. When I was 10 years old, he received a job offer to work at the Washington Hospital Center, the largest private hospital in the nation's capital city. He accepted, and the position prompted a move for our family to Bethesda, Maryland, right outside the northwest tip of Washington, DC.

I started sixth grade after the move and dove into life in our new area. In a sense, I literally dove—into a pool. I took up swimming and went on to compete as an athlete in college, at Colgate University. When selecting a major, I chose English (during those years, there was no real estate program available). I found time to study between swim meets, and eventually went on to become captain of the swim team.

While I could maneuver my way around team sports, competition, and what it took to get a liberal arts education, I didn't have a strong direction toward the future as graduation neared. At the start of the spring semester during my senior year, I was still trying to figure out what exactly I was going to do once school ended. Options abounded. I tossed around the possibility of moving to the West Coast to make movies. That had a strong appeal . . . until I learned no one was willing to pay me a salary to create films! Also, I didn't have any money to get started on my own.

MY FIRST REAL ESTATE JOB

I knew some of my friends were going to New York City to work after college, so I decided to check out the jobs available there. During March of my senior year, I went to the Career Service Center on the Colgate campus with a copy of my resume in hand and asked about job openings.

As it turned out, Massey Knakal, an investment-sales brokerage in New York City, had a posting there. The firm, which was founded in 1988 by Robert Knakal and Paul Massey, was looking for a sales associate. The job posting included a deadline for applying, which happened to be the very day I was in the career center! I asked if a cover letter was needed to show I was interested in the position. The answer? "No, just a copy of your resume." Fortunately, I still had that copy on hand; I quickly dropped it in the appropriate box for the job posting.

To my immense surprise—given that I had virtually no background in real estate—a week later the company called me and requested an in-person interview. We set a date, and when I went to New York for the interview, I was taken aback by the city's size and grandeur. I had been in the sprawling metropolis a couple of times before, as my roommate in college was from New Jersey. On visits to his home, he had taken me around New York City, but this was the first time I ventured in on my own. I walked up to the office for Massey Knakal, which was impressively located on luxurious Park Avenue.

During the interview, my knowledge about real estate was confirmed, which consisted of nothing beyond my observations of my grandfather's dealings! Fortunately, they were willing to look at some other aspects of my background, including my leadership on the swim team and willingness to work hard. So, I was hired.

A week later, I learned that I was actually their second choice. Only two people had applied for the position, and they had first offered the job to the other candidate, who accepted. Then they decided they wanted one more associate and resolved to take a chance on me.

Perhaps it was meant to be: I had a great vibe about the place from the very first handshakes with the owners. The first hire lasted six months. I ended up staying at Massey Knakal for 17 years, becoming a partner and helping build the company which became the #1 sales firm in NYC. We ultimately sold to Cushman & Wakefield for approximately $100 million dollars. I had three great years there alongside my partners, until I was given an incredible opportunity to build out Avison Young's investment sales team.

From day one of the job, I knew I was in the right place. Under the title of broker for the firm, I set out on foot to get to know my area. Massey Knakal had developed a territory system in which they divided up New York City into 50 sections; each broker covered a specific neighborhood. Mine consisted of Chelsea, a dense, residential quarter with restaurants, bars, cafes, and parks. I was tasked with getting to know every owner, every sale that took place, and everything else that was going on in the section. Like my associates, I went from one building to the next, taking pictures of each property. We would place the photos, along with other information about the location, in a three-ring binder we called the owners' book.

Soon immersed into the fast-paced, highly intense real estate scene, I found myself competing against seasoned brokers who had 20 or more years of experience in the business. Despite the tough competition, I brought in clients to our brokerage firm and owners started asking me to oversee the sales of their properties.

The key to my quick success lay in my eagerness to learn and become an expert. I knew more about my assigned neighborhood than brokers from competitive firms who were present in the space but acted as generalists. They knew a little bit about a lot of things. I, on the other hand, became a source of insider information on Chelsea, as I had knowledge that few others did. It gave me an advantage over others, simply because I could share tips, such as the most recent sales, new retailers coming to the area, up-and-coming developments, and recent changes to the zoning codes (zoning refers to the laws and regulations in a city that govern how a property can be used).

Let's pause for a moment here, as you may be thinking: "James, isn't this supposed to be about real estate investing? Don't brokers oversee the transacting and not the investing?"

Let me explain. Yes, my career has consisted of being a broker in my day job and helping owners sell buildings. Like my grandfather, however, I have made my own investments over the years. I have purchased and sold properties as an investor and monitored my own returns. Unlike my grandfather, I have been an eyewitness to the inner workings of both buyers and sellers and have the benefit of an extensive network in New York City. I have picked up insider knowledge through these experiences and my connections with other highly successful investors.

It must be said that when I'm working as a broker with a seller, helping them through the sale of a property, I don't put on my buyer's hat, as that would create a direct conflict of interest. In a similar way, when I'm helping a buyer go through the transaction of purchasing a property, I put the buyer's needs first and don't issue my own bids. This code of ethics spans across the industry for brokers, as expectations are set that we are prioritizing our client's preferences and not imposing our own interests.

As you learn more about buying and selling properties (or may already be aware), you'll see that many brokers, myself included, do make real estate investments. I occasionally have an opportunity to buy if a different broker is representing a seller, for instance. Or

I might form a partnership with another investor, and that person will oversee the purchasing and managing of the property. Again, in these instances, I avoid conflicts of interest with clients who come to me for broker services.

Getting back to my story, after starting as a broker for Massey Knakal, I went on to join Avison Young. There I became principal and head of the firm's Tri-State Investment Sales Group, leading a group involved in the sale of multifamily, retail, office, and development properties throughout the country.

INSIGHTS, KNOWLEDGE, AND TENACITY

As I reflect on my career, I'm deeply thankful for the individuals and firms that held out a hand and helped me along this journey. I've been involved in some fantastic deals and gained new insight at every step. I've learned tough lessons from watching an occasional opportunity slip by, but I've also followed my grandfather's logic and moved on, applying new strategies to the next deals based on those less-than-ideal experiences.

Having this inside seat both as a broker and investor has allowed me to analyze countless investment properties, underwritings, well-thought-out business plans, and deal structures. Since my firm values hundreds of properties every year, I can very quickly identify if a building is being acquired for less than its market value—or more. (This is essential to understand how to outperform the market.)

I've worked with a long list of brokers, investors, attorneys, architects, designers, contractors, managers, and other real estate professionals, and spoken in depth with many of them to understand their personal challenges and success stories. On the investment side, I've had the privilege to partner with other investors in dozens upon dozens of opportunities, which has enabled me to see how different players operate and interact in this industry.

The more experience I rack up in real estate, the clearer it becomes to me that it takes more than having a knack for numbers or being able to invest large amounts of personal wealth to get great outcomes. To outperform the market, there's a stroke of creativity needed. I personally love to dig in and think about innovative ways to view an existing or upcoming property. The only limitation is your city's zoning perimeters, which can sometimes be amended. If you can dream up a new plan—or work with someone who can—you could add value to a place and be compensated for those ideas.

I've carried out this strategy time and again . . . so often, in fact, that I've established a reputation for finding great opportunities and working with the right team to reposition a property and outperform the market. My partners at Massey Knakal launched a fund with RiverOak, an established asset management firm. This fund essentially allowed others to contribute anywhere from $100,000 to $2.5 million and pool their contributions to invest in value-add investments in New York City. I worked with partners to raise two successful funds, totaling around $50 million in equity that we ended up investing in over 30 properties with an overall capitalization of around $350 million.

All these investments, and the chance to view an ongoing stream of transactions go across my desk, has been a fascinating, invigorating journey for me. I share my story to show that the possibilities are out there, and that you don't need a certain set of credentials to get started (I certainly did not!). My path to success has greatly been generated by my willingness to learn and move forward.

During my time in real estate, I've found that fear can hold back would-be investors. They aren't sure if an investment is a great opportunity, if the property will generate a return, if they'll be able to raise the money needed, and so on. I'm here to say that for those that look at real estate investing as a way to solve problems and find a solution, the opportunities are endless. Even if things don't work out perfectly, you can find a way to move on and try again—keep swinging, so to speak, and you'll eventually hit that home run.

In addition to recalling my grandfather's dealings, one phrase he often repeated will always stick with me. He said, "The most important thing for success is tenacity." His words, as they did back in my early years, still ring true today. Not every step will go smoothly, but having the determination to work through challenges will equip you with the right skill set for this space.

Furthermore, my goal with telling my story—and writing this book—is to give you the resources needed to get started, understand the basics, dispel any fears, and be inspired to set out on your own path. During my years in this space, I've learned that it's an insider's game: who you know matters. I've also found that it's not easy to discover all the information you need to become successful. That's why I'm eager to lay it out here and share both my experiences and knowledge with others who want to pursue their own investments and build their own legacies. When you do, I invite you to reach out to me and share your own story. My guess is that it will be just as exciting and fascinating as my grandfather's, and the very stories I've experienced and recounted in the pages that follow.

ACKNOWLEDGMENTS

First, I would like to thank Paul Massey and Bob Knakal, who welcomed me into this incredible business in 1998. Even though we joke that I was your second choice out of two candidates, you gave me a shot when I had no experience. I, along with so many others, have learned the right way by you. It was my true pleasure to be your partner for the first 20 years of my career and friends for life.

Next, I have to thank my friend Ryan Serhant for inspiring me to write this book and to always step up my game. You are a true force who always delivers. I am very appreciative of your Foreword, and for introducing your world to *The Insider's Edge to Real Estate Investing*.

Along the way, I have had so many incredible mentors and coaches. Rod Santomassimo, Blaine Strickland, and Mike Gallegos have taught me and so many other real estate professionals how to be at the top of our games.

I would like to thank Steve DeNardo and Derek Eakin from RiverOak, our cofounders of two real estate funds. So much of the wisdom of this book came from our deals. A special thanks to Derek, who also contributed to a chapter and shared his expertise in reviewing this book.

There are so many wonderful organizations that I have been privileged to be a part of, including The Colgate Real Estate Council, CRE, ICSC, REBNY, RESA, ULI, and YM/WREA. I have met so many amazing people through your networks, like my good friend Bill Montana, who always looks out for me!

I am extremely thankful to Donya and the team at McGraw Hill. It is a thrill to partner with them on this exciting project and I am so appreciative of their global publishing platform.

I'd like to thank Kevin Anderson & Associates for everything you have done to make this book a reality, especially introducing me to my writing partner, Rachel Hartman. We have had so much fun along the way. I'm not sure she knew what she was in for when she said yes! Thanks also to Ryan and Charlie from Very Social and my marketing team for helping get the word out! A special nod to John Santoro for his excellent contribution with graphics for the book.

I'm excited to have the backing of Smith Publicity and Book Highlight, whose incredible team has worked diligently to create awareness and get this book into the hands of readers.

I would not have been able to accomplish any of this without my incredible team and family at Avison Young. Erik and Brandon, it is a true honor and pleasure to have you as partners and be with you each day. To Mitch and David, who have been by my side all these years; to Alex, my right hand; to Eireen, who I never thank enough; and to all the wonderful members of the Tri-State Investment Sales team. You inspire me each day. To Mark Rose, our CEO, who truly leads by example, and to Dorothy, for all you do for our New York office.

To all my clients whom I have learned so much from and all the incredible legends who have shared your wisdom on my podcast, I send my heartfelt gratitude.

Finally, I want to thank my family for all your support over the years. To my wife, Allison, who is the most loving and selfless person I know, and my sons, Luke, Austin, and TJ, who are my greatest joy. You give me the energy to go out and be the best I can be each day.

To my parents and brother, George, for always believing in me, I say thank you. To the Amens for everything you do, I am so grateful. To say that I'm lucky is an understatement.

Most importantly, I want to thank you, the reader, for your support. It is my true hope that this book inspires you to take action with the *Insider's Edge*. If we haven't met, I hope our paths will cross someday soon!

INTRODUCTION

I f I told you the US real estate investment market is valued at nearly $21 trillion, and nearly half of the properties on that market were purchased by individual investors, would you be surprised?[1] These numbers don't always make the headlines, but they reveal an important opportunity. Clearly, there is a wide selection of property available for those who are prepared and well equipped to jump in.

Better yet, take note of the term "individual." You don't need to be a large corporation, a founder of an equity firm, or part of a real estate investing company to take part in these deals. While substantial players certainly are active in the market, there's plenty of space that can be taken up by a single person, someone investing with a partner, and really, any individual interested in making the leap into real estate investing in the United States.

During my more than 20 years of experience in the US real estate industry, I've met a long list of incredibly successful investors who saw the chance to participate in the market—and after starting, many times from ground zero, they built their way up to accrue fortunes, created a legacy, and even had the chance to give back to their communities and the charities close to their heart. Their efforts took time and plenty of grit, not to mention a bit of risk—which is inherent in any type of investment. Although their individual experiences are unique, they tend to share a common thread that mirrors my own story. For those with an inside edge, the sky is really the limit in terms of the rewards you can reap from real estate investing.

When I began my real estate career, I hit the pavement and worked my area in New York City until I knew it like the back of my hand. As the deals came, I put my research into action and went after the ones to which I could add value. Along the way, I built up an intricate network and made friends with everyone from New York's wealthiest families to the superintendents sweeping outside the apartment buildings in my neighborhood. I learned the ropes and built experience as a broker, which gave me the chance to view or be involved in thousands of deals and participate in more than $5 billion worth of sales. I've been an investor myself and have spearheaded funds to allow others to do the same.

REAL ESTATE OFFERS BETTER OPPORTUNITIES THAN STOCKS

Here's what I've learned: when it comes to real estate investing, the field tends to be opaque and inefficient. Unlike other types of investments such as stocks and bonds, it's not easy to see all the options available and carry out transactions quickly. With stocks, you can pull up listings on the site of your choice and see how your selection (or the investment you're considering) has performed in the past. You might read about the company, follow the numbers, and even take into account forecasts that lay out future expectations. And guess what? Everyone else who visits those sites has the same information. In a sense, this makes stocks more transparent. It puts us all on a level playing field, where we share common knowledge.

Now, I can control how I invest my funds in the stock market or talk to my wealth advisor team about their recommendations, but that's about where my involvement ends. I won't be sitting in on a board meeting, getting the inner scoop that is hidden to the public eye. In fact, the law prohibits insider trading. In that sense, if you or I know too much, we could in theory be facing a legal discussion, which of course we don't want! Instead, we line up with the other players and watch the stock market click along in this open arena.

If the stock market were a hand of poker, it might be one in which we all saw each other's hands. Real estate investing, at its essence, is a completely different game. It's a bit more like the poker interaction we're more familiar with, the one where everyone holds their cards close to their chest. How do you know what cards the person to your left is holding? It's up to you to figure it out.

There's no complete listing that lays out all the possible real estate investments in a particular area. While you might use Zillow or Trulia when shopping for a residential home, there is no single site available online where you can find all the apartment buildings, office spaces, condominium complexes, and industrial centers that are on the market. What you find will be incomplete listings or a handful of options available to the public through different sources such as brokers. There are many properties out there, every day, that are not listed for all to see but are very much on the market—you just have to know where to find them.

And that is part of the magic of real estate investing. If you have the inside edge, you'll be able to, first and foremost, locate the deals available. You'll also have the knowledge needed to identify the gems, build the right team with whom you'll make and manage the investments, and then take the properties to the next level, either by renovating them or thinking creatively about how they could be positioned in the market. Once you've put in the legwork, you can decide if it's best to sell and re-invest to uplevel your game, or keep the income-generating assets while hunting for more.

If you're new to this game, you might be wondering how you can get into this space. You may not have experience or even have the deposit money required to do a transaction. Let me assure you: the most important thing you can bring to the real estate table is a deal. In most markets, there are always more buyers than sellers. Finding the great opportunities is the hard part. If you can discover these, you can bring in a partner and move forward (and I'll tell you how to do exactly that in the chapters to come).

This process is exciting, and it brings in a whole new set of possibilities to the investing space. While I would argue that other opportunities, including the stock market, mutual funds, and 401(k) accounts certainly have their place in a diversified portfolio, real estate stands out as way to build massive wealth on your own terms. Whether you have $25,000 or $1 million to invest, there are plenty of ways to put those dollars to work in properties and generate income. In addition, thanks to tools and resources today such as crowdfunding, there are ways to invest smaller amounts, meaning the playing field is more open and the barrier to entry is lower than ever.

There's another aspect of real estate that can generate wealth growth, and it lies in the ability to leverage your investment. Think of the mortgage on a home, in which the buyer offers a down payment and takes out a loan. Perhaps the home's sale price is $1,000,000 and the purchaser puts in 30 percent, or $300,000, as a down payment, and then takes out a loan for $700,000. The individual now has an asset worth $1,000,000, with only contributing $300,000 to the investment. If the property appreciates, the bank is not participating in that upside. (Unfortunately, the bank doesn't share in your losses if the property drops in value!)

For investment property, you also receive the benefits of cash flow. If you finance an investment, and the property generates a higher return (known as a capitalization rate, which we'll get to in Step 5) than the interest rate on the loan, then you'll benefit from a positive cash-on-cash return (another point we'll discuss in-depth in Step 5). Once the value of the property has increased, you can refinance out some or all your equity. Finally, there are incredible tax advantages to investing in real estate. A substantial one is a 1031 exchange where you can defer your gains into another like-kind investment.

(Like-kind is an industry term which refers to properties that are of the same nature or character; they could differ in grade or quality though.) Think of these investments like a spiral going up: after initial transactions, you can potentially purchase higher-priced assets, which lead to more returns, and so on.

Given the substantial opportunities in today's real estate investing market, you might think the space is overloaded with investors. In my experience, I've found the opposite is true: few take advantage of the deals—and profits—that could be made. The majority simply don't know how to find great value and make a dream of real estate investing turn into a reality.

You can change those statistics, and it starts with becoming an insider. That's what this book is about, and in its pages, I'll outline the steps to follow. The setup is simple and straightforward: there are 10 steps, and each chapter focuses on 1 step. I will try to be as specific as possible with real examples, so you will know precisely what to do. By traveling down the path I lay out, there are deals to be made, profits that could skyrocket, and a lasting legacy to be generated. Let's get started.

STEP 1
Find the Right Property Type

I n the mid-1990s, Sam Zell bought a mobile home park. At the time, practically no other real estate investors were interested in mobile homes, which made it easy for Sam to keep buying more. His focus paid off: in 2016 alone, his company Equity Lifestyle Properties, the largest owner of mobile home lots in the United States, made $869 million.[1]

Of particular significance is that Sam didn't have an extraordinary advantage over others in the real estate market when he began his journey to building a fortune. He didn't have a specialized background or an ultraprivileged education. Sam's parents immigrated to the United States shortly before Germany invaded Poland in 1939. Their route took them through Japan, and they arrived in America in 1941. Sam was born just 90 days later,[2] and the family settled in Chicago, where Sam's father worked as a jewelry wholesaler.[3]

One lesson that Sam's parents emphasized during his growing years was to work hard and strive to move up and build a better life.[4] This trait stuck with him as he entered early adulthood and took on his first jobs.

During his college years at the University of Michigan, Sam and a friend managed student apartment units for a landlord. He went on to purchase and sell his own properties, flipped some homes, and explored different types of real estate investments in the years following college.[5] You might say that during this time, he built up his inside knowledge of real estate. This insight, learned through experience, eventually led to his discovery of mobile home parks, a relatively underrecognized investment during the 1980s and 1990s.

INSIDER TIP

Finding your niche in real estate investing begins with understanding what property type best suits you along with the right management intensity and risk levels. Your knowledge of area developments, comparable sales, and the demand drivers will give you the advantage.

You don't have to follow in Sam's shoes, but we can all glean several lessons from his story. First, there's value in starting small and working with a partner (in Sam's case, his friend) to understand the inner workings of the real estate industry. You'll almost certainly be involved with a partner on your first deal, and this person should be someone you know and trust. We'll cover that more in Step 2. Second, once you find the right property type, you can jump in and look for ways to add value and accumulate more properties. Finally, you can diversify as you go; in other words, you can branch into different property types as you proceed down the path of real estate investing.

It all begins with an initial investment and choosing a property type. Glance around your neighborhood and you'll likely be able to start a list. If you're located in a city, you might see multifamilies, office buildings, retail, medical, industrial, and land for sale. This plethora of real estate can be grouped into sections called asset classes. When we talk about real estate investing, an asset class, also known as a property type, refers to a group of products that share common features; they also frequently perform in a similar way on the market. The four main asset classes for real estate investing are: multifamily, retail, office, and land.

It's important to understand what's involved in each property type before you get started. In addition, as you search, you'll want to make sure you're not overextending yourself and your finances. By putting in the correct safeguards, you can get off on the right foot. Let's walk through the different asset classes and discuss how to find the best fit for your comfort zone.

ASSET CLASS #1: MULTIFAMILY

As its name suggests, a multifamily or apartment building is a residential property that contains more than one housing unit. If you own this type of property and live in one of the units, it's typically called a live plus investment property. As an asset class, multifamily includes duplexes, townhouses, condominiums, and apartment buildings. Really, any building that is divided for two or more households is considered a multifamily property.

In the real estate investment industry, multifamily properties can come in many shapes and forms. Purchasing a small duplex in a quiet suburban neighborhood will not be the same as financing a 40-unit apartment building in the heart of downtown. Everything from the purchase costs to the management needs of properties in this asset class vary greatly.

When speaking about real estate, I always emphasize the advantages that come with starting small. Many investors choose to begin by securing a residential loan for a multifamily property with four or fewer units. They live in one of the units and rent the remaining ones. By doing this, they are able to often receive a higher "loan to value" (the loan amount divided by the value of the property—see more about this term in Step 6). They can nearly always offset their living expenses with the rental income. Along the way, they can learn about managing tenants, overseeing the building, and what it is like to live in one of the units. That said, the focus in this book lies in larger investments that include multifamilies with over five units.

When multifamily properties have five or more units, I always point out to investors that the management of the property may exceed their time availability and their repair and upkeep capabilities. Even if you live in one of the 10 apartments in a building you own, you have to think about the time factor. Do you have a full-time job? Are you able to respond to every tenant call, both day and night? Are you handy and interested in carrying out repairs? In many cases, you'll need to take on professionals to help you maintain and run the place.

INSIDER TIP

Always think about the highest and best use for a multifamily investment. Could you turn a single-family townhouse into multiple units or convert a multiunit place back to a single-family home? It depends on what's most in demand in your area.

Multifamily is by far the largest asset class in the real estate market throughout the country. It accounts for the majority of the dollar volume, year after year.[6] In 2021, the sales volume for apartment properties amounted to more than $340 billion. In comparison, the sales volume for office, retail, and land for development totaled around $145 billion, $81 billion, and $32 billion, respectively. The same is true for the number of properties sold: multifamily again leads the way here. In 2021, more than 13,000 apartment properties were sold. Compare this to around 6,500 sales for offices; nearly 10,000 for retail; and just over 3,000 sales of land for development.[7]

One of the reasons multifamily investments may be appealing, generally speaking, is that they are viewed as somewhat conservative in terms of risk. If you lose a tenant, you can set out to find another, and you still have other tenants who are paying their rents. Compare this to a freestanding retail or office property that has just one tenant. If that tenant leaves, and you still have a mortgage to pay, you could be reaching into your pocket to cover the debt service if the place doesn't fill quickly. In contrast, with a multifamily unit, you need to offer fewer concessions, or enticements, to attract renters and the costs associated with re-tenanting usually are less than retail or office properties. With retail or office, the landlord often pays a tenant improvement (TI) allowance so that the renter can fix up the place for their business purposes and may endure extensive down-time while changes are made.

ASSET CLASS #2: RETAIL

Whether you live around the corner from a gas station, 30 miles from a restaurant, or somewhere in between, it's easy to see how retail supports our existence and livelihood. In this asset class, you'll find everything from small mom-and-pop shops to home improvement box stores, sprawling malls, supermarkets, and more. Some are incredibly specialized, such as a doctor's office or a hair salon; others can be more general in form and use.

Arrangements with tenants in this asset class can differ drastically, depending on your space and renter. There are many smaller players, such as family-owned dry-cleaning businesses, local restaurants, and barber shops, many of which are characterized as service retail. This type of tenant can bring a certain level of risk, as they don't come with strong guarantees that you might get from a national tenant. It could be hard for the tenant to pay rent if the dry-cleaning business goes through a dry stretch (pun intended).

Retail also encompasses larger players, such as national brands or major corporations with stores throughout the country. We typically refer to these bigger clients as credit tenants, which means they are considered to have exceptional credit. Rating agencies such as Moody's or Dun & Bradstreet can be used as a resource to determine the strength of these companies. There is a high assurance they will pay on time, every time.

If you see a CVS or a Walgreen's at the corner near your house, these shops are not usually owned by the parent company. Instead, an investor generally owns these properties and leases them to the corporation. Many of these were created with sale-leasebacks. After the company acquires and builds the site, they sell the property to a different owner, who then leases it back to them. This allows the company to spend their capital on growing the business as opposed to owning the real estate.

There are five main types of commercial leases: full-service, net, modified gross, absolute NNN, and percentage. They differ in the way they divide the expenses related to the property. Here's a quick breakdown of each:

- **Full-service lease.** Also called a gross lease, under this arrangement the tenant pays a base rent. The landlord covers additional building expenses, such as maintenance fees, insurance, and real estate taxes.
- **Net lease.** A lease in which the tenant pays a portion of the building's operating expenses. They might help cover maintenance in common areas, property taxes, and insurance. There are three types of net leases: single, double, and triple.

For a single net lease, the tenant pays for rent and utilities plus property taxes; with a double net lease, the tenant pays for rent and utilities plus property taxes and building insurance; under a triple net lease, the tenant pays for rent and utilities plus property taxes, building insurance, and all other operating expenses.

- **Modified gross lease.** A commercial lease that is in between the full-service lease and a triple net lease. It usually means that the tenant pays base rent, utilities, and part of the operating costs for the property.
- **Absolute NNN lease.** A commercial lease in which the tenant is responsible for all expenses related to the building, including maintenance and repairs to the property's structure. In these cases, the tenant virtually owns the property without having the buy it.
- **Percentage lease.** A commercial lease in which the tenant pays a base rent along with a percentage of the gross business sales. This percentage is typically paid once a certain threshold has been met.

When it comes to investing, securing financing for a retail space is frequently more complex and requires a higher level of funds to get started. That said, the rents on retail are often higher than what you'll find in small multifamily properties. While this can come across as appealing, it also brings added risk.

For starters, it can be difficult to find a tenant, especially if the plot and building are designed for one clientele profile. If you lease a space to a dentist who decides after a year to move into a bigger space, you'll have to either find another dentist interested in moving in or you'll be looking at some major rework to accommodate a new client in a different industry. Even if you have another dentist come in as a tenant, there may be some adjustments that have to be made to fit their specialty.

While it's worth discussing retail in general, it's true that many restaurants and stores closed their doors during the pandemic. There's also the ongoing trend for consumers to shop online and have goods delivered right to their doorstep. In light of these happenings, questions have been raised about the future of retail. Clearly, change is in the air, and the retail industry will continue to evolve and shift in new ways during the coming years. Still, it's important to point out that this asset class hasn't disappeared, and it does continue to provide a customer experience that online marketplaces like Amazon can't replicate.

For those who are just beginning to invest in real estate, I would stay away from single tenant, noncredit retail properties. Multitenant is certainly safer. An alternative could be a mixed-use property which has retail on the ground and residential above to offset some of the risk if your retailer vacates.

> **INSIDER TIP**
>
> Having a retail tenant in hand that wants to expand can be a way to build a fortune in this business. You could buy vacant retail property at a discount, and then finance it as leased, with your new tenant signing a lease simultaneously to your purchase.

ASSET CLASS #3: OFFICE

When looking at an office building, I always point out that you need to be well-capitalized. By that I mean you'll need to have access to enough resources, either of your own or with other investors and financing, to be able to operate without severe monetary constraints. Here's why: office buildings, in short, are expensive, especially when compared to other asset classes.

The property may be in solid condition, but even if that's the case, you'll be looking at costs to improve the place for clients. There may be minor work, such as painting and bathroom upgrades, to carry out. However, it's not uncommon for massive renovations to be needed, especially as companies morph into hybrid working environments and require different spaces for employees, when they do come into the office.

Keep long-term trends in mind when considering an office investment. A lot of controversy about the topic arose after the downfall of WeWork, a shared working space that went from a value of $47 billion to around $9 billion when it went public in 2021.[8] However, many of their locations remain. There are also a variety of coworking companies that will either lease your entire building for you or manage one on your behalf.

Since there is so much involved with buying an office building and getting it ready for tenants, along with costs associated with signing tenants, the time frame for returns on investments with this asset class tends to be lengthy. It's not unusual for two years to pass without any income coming in.

Then there is the management aspect. Running a property with several offices (or more) requires a strong partner. You'll need someone who can maintain both the building and the tenants. There will be ongoing repairs and improvements that will need to be carried out from year to year too.

INSIDER TIP

Think about the future of work trends before you delve into office ventures. Since the pandemic, the way people work has radically changed, from hybrid workweeks to relocations across the country. This phenomenon is evolving, so it must be considered carefully before making long-term bets.

Investors who take on office buildings are usually very sophisticated and have deep pockets. There will generally be a strong capital partner involved in the project too. They will take the long view, which is good, because it may be years before they start to see a return. For these reasons, office isn't usually a top-of-the-list item for first-time investors. Again, we'll go more into the opportunities in this space later in the book.

ASSET CLASS #4: LAND

Often called "development," this is an asset class that appeals mostly to experienced, highly capitalized investors. It focuses on land and construction. That said, it's certainly worth listing here so we can see our options. There's a long process to follow, which starts with getting a project approved and then overseeing the construction. Of course, there is the financial aspect too, which often involves signing personal guarantees and thus adds to the risk.

For this reason, I don't usually advise those who are merely beginning in this space to forge into acquiring land and building on it. There's just too much that can go awry. Something can happen beneath the ground before the project even starts. There are a million additional ways it can derail during the construction process too.

Then there's the timeline risk to think about. You'll have high up-front costs that won't start to get reimbursed, let alone turn a profit, until after the construction is complete, the interior is finalized, and the tenants are inside—and paying. That doesn't mean you should always avoid the development property; it's an area you can definitely consider later—and we'll cover it in subsequent pages. This discussion is worth revisiting when you have the financial freedom to expand and do not feel the pressure of an immediate paycheck.

> ### INSIDER TIP
>
> If you are going to develop for the first time, make sure it is a "shovel ready" site, meaning it is set for you to get started with approved plans and environmental reports satisfied. I have seen horror stories where sites sit for well over a decade as they wait for approvals to go through.

UNDERSTAND THE RISK PROFILES

In addition to asset classes, another way to sort out where to make your first footprint when investing is to evaluate your risk tolerance. By using a lens of cost versus benefits, we can look at different kinds of opportunities, some of which span various property types. There are terms attached to these risk levels, and the main ones are: core investment, core plus, value-add, and opportunistic.

Core Investment

If you make a core investment, it means you take on a property that typically comes "ready to go." A tenant will already be settled into the premises, meaning you don't have to go find a renter—or pay someone else to bring you one. Moreover, the property usually has a credit tenant, which, as we discussed, is one that has a strong financial record.

A core investment is considered to have the lowest risk of the four categories and is often a great fit for passive investors. In these arrangements, you usually don't have to do much except collect the paycheck every month. They frequently operate as a "triple net," which, as mentioned, means that the tenant pays the rent, utilities, property taxes, building insurance, and all other operating expenses.

This is a solid starting point for investors who want a safe return and low risk. The drawback is that the potential return opportunities are not as high as some of the other categories. Furthermore, the return is usually consistent over a long-term contract. If the lease is for 10 years with a 6% return, and then four years into the deal, inflation zips upward and reaches 8%, that return you were planning on could evaporate into thin air. To offset this, there are long-term leases that are inflation protected. These might offer additional rent increases based on upticks in the Consumer Price Index (CPI), which measures inflation.

Core Plus

When we consider this risk category, we're often looking at an asset that is already cash flowing, meaning it is producing income when you buy it. There may also be some chances to fix it up and add value. You might buy a five-unit apartment building that was constructed in the 1980s or 1990s. It has tenants in it that are faithfully paying rent, but the interior could use some freshening up. Maybe you go in and renovate the kitchens and bathrooms. You usually won't be carrying out extensive construction projects, like gutting the building or tearing it down and starting from scratch.

This is a great segment of the market for a first-time investor to consider. You don't have to do heavy construction or repositioning. There is more upside potential here than with a core investment since you can make changes to add value and potentially increase the rents. Still, there will be more risk with these properties: for example, the tenants probably won't have that outstanding credit that comes with a core investment. Also, you might have to put in a bit more money up front to make renovations.

Value-Add

This, my friends, is where a professional investor spends a lot of their time. When you think of adding value, the picture changes. There is often an issue or challenge that has to be faced and solved before you can get a return. There may not be income coming from the place, or you might have to spend heavy amounts to get it in better shape, which translates to higher risk and greater up-front costs.

Perhaps you come across a retail space that hasn't rented for years. You might do major renovations, such as reimagining the property and putting in a totally new interior or building out a restaurant. Maybe an apartment building has large, oversized apartments with a lot of wasted space. Taking a one bedroom and converting it to a two bedroom might yield a lot more rent and strong return on investment (ROI).

The problem could consist of tenancy issues, such as renters who aren't paying or are sending in amounts every month that are below the market average. You may need to ask tenants who aren't paying at all to leave. This might, in some cases, involve having to evict certain tenants and bring in new ones. You could then go through the process of revamping the property and bringing in renters who are willing to pay more.

This category is where some of the biggest opportunities lie. You can add value to places where there are problems by bringing solutions. Maybe the seller is aware of what needs to be done but doesn't want to deal with the hassle. You can come in, make the needed changes, and then pass it on to another investor.

Suppose you buy a place that is listed as having a 4% return and you know the rents are below market. You think you can get them up to a 6% or 7% return, which would be your stabilized return on investment. Once you get the property fixed and have tenants settled, the place could generate much more cash flow. At this point, you can hand it over on a silver platter to someone like a core investor who is willing to pay more for a place in exchange for having someone—that person being you—who has already taken care of the hard work for them.

Opportunistic

This generally refers to heavy development, such as tearing down a building and erecting a new one. These investments bear the most risk. Still, they also yield a potentially higher return than the other categories.

Investors in projects that require so much heavy lifting are often looking for returns in the mid- to high teens. They start with a property that is generating no cash flow. Then they pour a lot of money into it to cover construction costs and to bring in tenants. If they've successfully added value and turned the place into a great income-generating opportunity, they'll likely sell it to another investor for a higher price. That's how they get those returns such as 15% or 19%, at least, as long as everything goes as planned.

These returns are representative over the life of the investment, including the ultimate sale, and are calculated as the internal rate of return, or IRR (more on this in Step 5). If something goes wrong, significant losses will follow. For this reason, it isn't a good fit for initial investors.

CLOSE TO HOME FOR THE WIN

Now that we've looked at the main asset classes for real estate investing and the risks to consider, we need to address the "where." There are cities and properties everywhere. How to choose? It can feel overwhelming when starting out and trying to narrow the options.

It doesn't have to be complicated. Think about your neighborhood for a moment. If you've lived there for some time, you intuitively have a significant advantage over others who aren't familiar with your region. That's because you know the streets a lot better than others.

For instance, suppose you have friends moving into your area and they're having a hard time finding a place to live because there aren't enough apartments available. Their issue could be a sign of an opportunity, such as more housing needed.

Is your downtown café always crowded? Perhaps there's room for another location to serve coffee to the overflow. Maybe city dwellers who used to work on-site but now are remote are looking for quiet neighborhoods far from the city center. Your sense of the town's culture, vibe, current events, living, and working situation collectively form your inside knowledge of the location.

INSIDER TIP

Leverage all the data that is available today and become the expert. If you study a sub-market for even 90 days you will know more about that area than 90% of the generalist investors with whom you'll compete and even some brokers who might not realize the true potential of what they're offering.

When you make a real estate investment close to home, you'll bring your expertise as a resident of the place to the table. If you add in partners, they'll take note of your knowledge, which will be viewed as a valuable component in the deal. Your investments can even outperform those of other investors who lack that local insight and grasp of the nuances at play. Of course, to get a step above competitors, you'll also want to understand zoning and other regulations in your area, all of which you can take the time to learn.

Being close has both short-term and long-term perks. You won't have to travel far to select your investments, and you can keep a careful eye on them as the project moves forward. If you're doing a renovation, for instance, you can check on the contractor to monitor progress on the site. Having that hands-on, day-to-day insight can help you make sure everything is done on the up-and-up.

One quick caveat on investing in your neighborhood: when I started in the business over 20 years ago, investors stayed in their lanes. They continuously invested close to home and in the same asset class. From a broker's perspective, it made our job easy, as the same group of buyers seemed to show up each time. Multifamily operators would buy apartment buildings in their specific neighborhoods. Retail investors with great tenant relationships bought in the same corridors. The office owners continued to grow their massive portfolios in their niche markets. We knew the developers who had the track records to borrow and build. I also don't remember buyers talking about other markets. Owners were proud that they could walk to their entire portfolio.

Things have changed. Post-Covid, real estate investing has been turned on its head. The hybrid work model has scattered employees and many real estate investors all over the country. This means experienced investors are branching into new property types, regions, and states. Consider the trend an opportunity for you in the future: you might begin in your town and eventually move into other cities and areas.

Ian Ross, founder and principal at SomeraRoad, a commercial real estate investment firm, took the approach of combining his expertise with a focus on location when he made his initial investments. His firm, which now operates in more than 70 unique markets throughout the country, continues to march to that drumbeat. To emphasize the need to know a neighborhood, Ian and his team hung a sign in their office reading "Know Thy Markets." When I interviewed him on my podcast, he reiterated the importance of being on the ground to know the inside pulse of a place. As he discussed the effort put in prior to an investment, he explained, "We toured neighborhoods, buildings, spent time at the restaurants and coffee houses, followed the sports teams . . . everything we could to understand the fabric and culture of a place."

When it comes to real estate investing the right way, there's simply no substitute for being able to go to the property once a week and see what is actually going on.

KEY TAKEAWAYS

- Your path to real estate investing begins with understanding which of the four main property types, often called asset classes, are most suitable for you: multifamily, retail, office, or land.

- Multifamily properties tend to be the most stable and accessible for beginning investors than other property types and can be a great way to get started and learn your way.

- When evaluating a potential property, look at its risk level, which is typically categorized as core investment, core plus, value-add, or opportunistic. This generally also defines how management intensive the investment will be.

- Start with locations and areas you know well to get an inside edge right away; you can always branch out later once you've gained some experience.

STEP 2

Know the Players

Pop quiz! If you spot an incredible deal, should you jump in with a bid? (Don't worry; I won't pass or fail you as a real estate investor based on your response.)

Answer: you shouldn't make a move until you have the right team in place. Here's why: if you see an opportunity that lines up with your risk tolerance and preferred type of property, when you reach out, you'll want to be ready to act on it right away.

As a lone investor, it can be hard to take all the next steps as they come up, including touring the property (which we'll get to later), setting up the financials (also coming soon!), and making an offer (of course, we'll get to this exciting step, too). All these processes tend to require the involvement of others, and you'll want to know who you can count on before they take place. For instance, who will tour the property with you? Who will help you raise capital? Which partners will also be in on the deal?

If you start the bidding process and haven't brought in others to help you lay the preliminary groundwork, things could get dicey—fast. That's because if you're not ready to move forward when you reach out, the selling broker and others will notice. And if they see you as an unprepared investor, that could cost you credibility. In this space, credibility is paramount and essential for building long-term relationships and securing deals. If you have a great reputation, brokers will want to work with you; if you don't, 9 times out of 10 they'll pass you over for someone else who is known to be a high performer and stands by their word.

Real estate investing is complicated, and while it may be fun to fantasize about bearing everything on our own shoulders, the reality is that much of your success will hinge on who is by your side. You'll often be working with one or more partners and will interact with many others along the way. So much of real estate depends on relationships, and who you know matters. In other words, if you have people you can turn to that have the inner track on properties you're interested in, you'll have a great advantage. Think of these individuals as A-players on your team. They'll help you find great opportunities, be ready to act when the time is right—and move forward in a smart, efficient way.

Several years ago, when I began my podcast, I interviewed Bruce Ratner, a New York City developer who has built over 50 projects, for my first episode.[1] He used the terms "team" and "people" more than 50 times during our one-hour conversation! Think about that for a moment. Bruce is a larger-than-life figure, and his name is tied to buildings that highlight the New York skyline. If you've seen a picture of New York City or visited the metro area, you've likely seen or stepped inside a project related in some form to Bruce. As chairman of Forest City Enterprises, a real estate development firm, he has overseen construction projects like the 700,000-square-foot New York Times building, the 929,000-square-foot MetroTech Center in downtown Brooklyn, and the Pacific Park project in downtown Brooklyn, which includes the Barclays Center for the NBA's Brooklyn Nets.[2] When he spoke to me, he could have pointed out his long line of achievements; instead, he emphasized how success came from having a team that provided the inside edge, which ultimately allowed him to orchestrate complex deals and build impressive structures. His success story really began with creating the right relationships with people.

Developing a team takes time and effort and can lead to invaluable results. Let's discuss who you need to know and why they're an important part of your real estate journey. We'll also delve into ways to find these people and get them on your side.

INSIDER TIP

Success is a team sport. Getting to know one specialist can put you in a position to get introduced to others. Things move quickly so don't wait until a deal to scramble and pull together a team.

THE TEAM PLAYERS

There are several categories of professionals whom I consider to be "must-haves" on your team. It's important to understand the different roles they will play as you move through the deal process. The following list might seem a bit extensive, but keep in mind that the right team members will help you find great value and increase your potential for returns.

You could gather in-depth, pivotal information from these players through routine everyday interactions. For instance, you may hear a leasing detail about a new restaurant that opened up down the block that gives you a competitive advantage while you're out for coffee with a retail leasing broker. An appraiser might tip you off about an estate sale that is about to happen. Or a land use attorney might tell you about a rezoning that is underway in a neighborhood while you're at a networking event. It's worth putting in the hours up front to form up a team that could produce a series of wins for everyone involved in this line of investing.

Sponsors

In a real estate project, the sponsor refers to the person or team that oversees all aspects of the acquisition process for the investors. You might also see terms such as general partner, operator, or syndicator used to describe this position. Their purpose is to spot properties that can produce a strong return. They'll be involved with developing a business plan, which is a document that outlines how the property will be used and how it will be managed. If there are other investors involved in the project, they are usually referred to as limited partners. The sponsor will often have more liability for the debt on the project than others that participate. This person will typically be you!

For investors, a top-notch sponsor can be a game changer when it comes to how the property is repositioned and the eventual return on investment. The sponsor works to reduce risk and optimize each step of the project. A sponsor will interact with the seller, the lender, the brokers, the investors, and others involved in the deal. The sponsor typically remains in partnership with the property for the entire time it's held.

A great sponsor might view one location and see an entirely different future for the space than another sponsor. For instance, with the shift to remote working, perhaps there are some neighborhoods outside of a city that are gaining residents, as workers move away from a downtown location. Maybe these employees, at one time, wanted to be near their office in the city center. Now, since they can work at home every day or some days of the week, they're looking for a quieter place where they can get away from a congested downtown and be near greener areas, thereby improving their quality of life.

There's just one problem. When these workers start looking for an apartment outside of the city, they realize they'd actually like a different type of living quarters to accommodate their new lifestyle. They want to work at home, but they would love to have a designated space that feels a bit more removed from their kitchen than a mere two footsteps to the home office.

Enter a sponsor with a quick eye, who sees an opportunity to get a great price for a four-story apartment building that could be renovated to create apartments and separate working spaces. The style could be called "live-work apartments" or "live-work condos." Or maybe they visualize a way to better close off one area of each apartment, to clearly distinguish between work and life. The sponsor could even decide to cater to home businesses and make apartments with extra storage for inventory and a landing space for supply deliveries. Maybe the place attracts makers who design and sell items on Instagram and need a spot for their different components. Someone might even have an at-home studio where they manufacture goods on a small scale and then ship them out to customers.

As you can see, the possibilities abound; it's a matter of getting creative and thinking about what could be, accounting for factors like market trends, resident interests, and investment costs and returns. Depending on your background, you might decide to be a sponsor or to work with one on a deal.

INSIDER TIP

If you have a passion for innovating, creative thinking, and envisioning change, you could be a sought-out sponsor. Investors will turn to you for your expertise and count on your unique outlook to create returns that outperform the market.

If you have years of experience in the investment arena, perhaps you feel you have a firm grip on some of the key aspects related to projects. Maybe you have a degree in architecture and opt to work with a sponsor who will oversee the processes while you contribute with unique design ideas. To learn about ways to add value, you might work with a sponsor who has been in the industry for several decades to see how it's done. There's nothing quite like on-the-ground experience to glean from others and build your own skill set in the real estate investing space.

Limited Partners

An individual, family office, fund, or private equity firm might participate in an investment on a passive basis. They aren't usually involved in the day-to-day decisions and all the details, but in many cases can have major decision-making rights, such as when to sell. The sponsor may send out regular communication or meet periodically with the limited partner or partners. If you come on to a project as a limited partner, it can be a great way to participate and observe how transactions are carried out. You'll typically have less liability tied to the debt than the sponsor or general partner.

Brokers

I might be biased(!), but I firmly believe a great team starts with knowing the right broker. A solid broker will understand the pulse of the marketplace and be able to inform you about what's going on. When you're looking at a property, they will be aware of the prices for which other similar buildings recently sold. They'll use their knowledge and experience from past deals to guide you in the right direction.

Most importantly—and this is key to getting the inside edge— they'll have access to great opportunities. They are oftentimes the gatekeepers to good deals, as they might hold listings that no one else does. A listing in the real estate investment segment is an agreement that names the broker to handle the sale of a property and receive a fee or a commission for their services. If you're following my logic, perhaps you'll agree with my potentially biased opinion: brokers often deliver properties that can generate great value, so you'll need to work with them to find out about these places and make a bid on them.

Before we get too far into a discussion on brokers, I want to clarify that there are different types of brokers. In my career, I spend my days as an investment sales broker, which I think is a perfect place to start with our definitions. Let's also run through other key broker titles you'll come across, including a selling broker, buyer broker, mortgage broker, and leasing broker (trust me, these are important, too, and I'll explain why below).

Investment Sales Broker

One key advantage that I have as an investment sales broker is the chance to see an ongoing stream of deals move across my desk. Like me, other investment sales brokers get a chance to compare one opportunity to another. After we've seen hundreds—or in my case, thousands—of deals, we're able to pick up nuances that don't readily meet the eye of someone with less experience.

Most times, we represent the seller exclusively in the sale of the property. We run a marketing process and aim to achieve the highest price. I'm making the case to perspective buyers so they can learn what it has to offer. I will suggest how to reposition the property or find untapped value like air rights, which refer to the right to build up to a certain point above a property and add on to the structure to increase its value.

There are also buyer brokers, but they are rare. Unlike residential sales, which might involve two brokers, there is usually one broker involved in the transaction. The seller's broker will find most of the buyers. That being said, in some cases there will be a buyer's broker in the transaction as well. Unfortunately, it is rare that brokers will represent a new buyer to the marketplace. You will likely have to approach the seller's broker directly or ask them for other opportunities that they know about.

The right investment sales broker will be aware of properties that might not be listed publicly but have been passed on to them as "off-market properties" (an industry term that means properties that aren't publicly listed). They can also keep their eyes and ears open for opportunities that match up with what you're interested in. A good investment sales broker is constantly in contact with others in the industry, keeping tabs on what's moving fast, what's hot, what's not, and where the good deals lie.

Here's a quick secret on the power behind a strong relationship with an investment sales broker. If you as an investor call me and want to ask about possible properties for sale, I'll never send you a bill for a phone call. That being said, you have to demonstrate that you are well informed and are serious about transacting. A broker only works for a commission, so time is money for them.

The difference here is that for many other professionals in real estate, such as attorneys and accountants, you'll be asked to pay a retainer to have some of those related conversations after an initial discussion. If you're going to get a bill that charges you for every hour you talk to them, I'm guessing you'll start choosing your words very carefully. In most cases, you're paying every time you pick up the phone to ask them a question, regardless of whether the deal goes through.

There's a reason brokers like myself tend to be willing to talk without charging. Our job is to bring sellers and buyers together, and orchestrating this act often requires a bit of problem-solving tactics.

I might have a property that I'm representing for a client, and I know that there's a tenant issue tied into the property. Or perhaps there's a problem with the certificate of occupancy that needs to be addressed. If I'm doing my work correctly, I'm going to help identify that situation up front with prospective buyers.

When people call me about a property with a tenant who is problematic, I'm going to share that information straight up. I might say,

"We're selling this building and it's a great opportunity; it's priced well below other comparable buildings on the market. But there's one problem we need to address. There's an issue with a tenant who is holding over and not paying rent. We're going to sell it as is, so you'll have to handle this."

Rather than ending the conversation there, I'll continue, "Don't worry, we've done a little research and I have some guidance I can share on the matter. By the way, we've got a landlord-tenant attorney." (We'll go over the role of a landlord-tenant attorney in the section on attorneys.) I'll conclude by saying, "They can help you figure this out."

Occasionally, I'll get an investor who calls me up and asks me what I consider to be an almost ideal question. "James," they'll say, "you see a lot of opportunities on the market. What would you be buying right now? What sort of business plans do you like to see?" This strategy is effective because it gives me the chance to share what might be some good ideas. Remember that we're having a free phone call.

You may hear something you like in your conversations with brokers or others in the industry that coincides with the type of property you want to secure. Who knows? After you hang up, you could get started on a business plan inspired by the conversation and try to implement it on a property. You might even call back to talk about properties that would be a good fit for what you've discussed and the plans you've drawn up.

INSIDER TIP

Connect with multiple sales brokers to find what they're working on and opportunities that they're seeing in the market. Ask them what's in their pipeline, not just what is listed or if they are aware of any off-market opportunities.

When working with brokers, keep in mind that the fees are success based. If you work with me to sell a property, there will typically be a commission when the property is sold. If you're represented by a buyer's broker, sometimes they will be compensated by the seller's broker. Other times, they'll ask you to pay their fee, provided it's disclosed and all parties are aware. If you're looking to invest in property, the commission will be tied to the transaction when the purchase goes through. This win-win atmosphere is to your advantage. Work with a broker who will help you find a great deal, and you'll both come out ahead.

Selling Broker

This is the broker working on the side of the seller in a transaction. As such, the broker will represent the best interests of the seller. They might contact parties who they think would be interested in the property, share information about it on social media, spread the word via other forms of communications like email messages and online listings, and highlight its features to all prospective buyers. A selling broker's job also includes educating the seller. For instance, they can inform the property owner of market conditions, what price to expect, when to wait, reasons to sell, and so on.

Buyer Broker

In this case, we have the broker working on the side of the buyer, and as such, they are "batting for the buyer," so to speak. They'll look for deals that might be of interest to the investor, research the market to understand pricing conditions, and help the buyer understand all there is to know about the property. An all-star buyer broker can help you view a location in an innovative way, such as looking at a vacant basement in an apartment building and determining if more units could be built to fill the space—and take in more rent income.

Mortgage Broker

As the name suggests, a mortgage broker helps coordinate lenders and borrowers for loan transactions. This individual won't use their own funds to provide the loans or service them; rather, they will connect a mortgage lender with you and your partners in the deal. If you are looking at a multifamily property with four or fewer units that you'll live in, you might qualify for a residential loan. This is the type of loan frequently used for homeowners, such as those purchasing a new residence or moving. You might have a loan on your home right now or be familiar with the process.

However, once you reach a multifamily property with five or more units, you'll need a commercial loan, which might be offered by a bank, a private lender, life insurance company, or even a securitized CMBS loan (see more about a CMBS loan in Step 6). The same is true for retail, office, and land properties.

This new category is a bit of a "whole new world" when it comes to loans. Unlike residential loans, which focus highly on your personal credit and earnings, the terms for commercial real estate loans are typically deal-specific, focusing on the financial performance of the property. In the commercial space, one loan can look vastly different from another, depending on the property, the owner, the partners, the financing sources, and plans for renovations or other changes to add value. The interest rate will depend on factors such as the tenancy of the property and the quality of the sponsor—remember I said reputation is everything—as well as the supplier of the loan (again, a nod to the emphasis on credibility in this space).

A great mortgage broker can walk you through your options and, better yet, find you the best ones for your situation and interests. Once you've chosen a property, the mortgage broker will take the case to lenders and ask for loan options. They might then sit down with you to compare multiple loan offers and guide you through understanding the language of the terms and next steps.

Leasing Broker

Suppose you spot a listing for a 10-unit apartment building. It looks like it's in good shape, and the price is a low basis compared to other sales in the area. In talking to your partners, you realize it's possible to add on 10 more units to the place. After the discussion, your imagination kicks into overdrive, and you start envisioning a rent roll coming in from 20 units—each month. A rent roll is a listing of all the rents due from tenants and which ones have been collected. It makes it easy to see the revenue that a property with tenants is generating. This could be huge, you think.

Not to put a damper on your plans, but I must point out a few caveats here. First and perhaps foremost, this question needs to be asked: Why is the price so low? Perhaps it's a family that owns the place and wants to get it off their hands. Or maybe there are some major repairs that must be carried out. If that's the case, you'll need to invest more to make the improvements. There could be other forces at play, too, which is exactly where a leasing broker can bring invaluable insight.

A leasing broker works to advise tenants and landlords during the leasing process. The leasing broker might advertise a rental space, show the unit to prospective tenants, help negotiate the lease for the place, and set up the lease signing. Given this, any leasing broker worth their salt will have inside knowledge regarding the market trends of the area. They'll know about demand and will specialize in a property type, such as apartments, retail, or office.

Following through with our example, if you work with a leasing broker who has expertise in apartments, that professional will know how much comparable units are renting for, the demographics of the tenants, and the ideal unit sizes. They'll also know if there is a strong demand in the area where the 10-unit (potentially 20-unit) building is located. They may advise that young professionals are moving into the area, and they are looking for places to share. You might have originally considered building out oversized family apartments, but the leasing broker could suggest you create efficient micro units. They will also coach you on the type of finishes or amenities needed in a building. You don't want to over-improve a property, but you also want to meet the demand to maximize rents. Will you need washers and dryers in the apartments, bike storage, and other features?

Together with the rental agent, you can determine what the best use is for the property to drive the highest rents per square foot.

That's exactly the type of information you'll get from a seasoned leasing broker, and let me assure you, it's not always a case of showing you the benefits. They can also advise of the warning signs, which could include an oversupply in a submarket (a submarket is a small section of a bigger market). In this case, they should be able to warn you about what types of concessions are being offered in the market. Is the new construction project across the street offering two months of free rent plus covering moving costs? Rental brokers could help you avoid making a big mistake.

Let's also point out before moving on that there are different types of leasing brokers. An office leasing broker helps negotiate terms with tenants in workplaces. A retail leasing broker will be an intermediary during the process of renting out store locales, shopping centers, and big box stores. An industrial leasing broker finds and negotiates with companies interested in warehousing space or production facilities.

There are other types of brokers as you get into more specialized areas. Don't let the long list overwhelm you. Instead, consider it a starting point to simply be aware that there are different players in this space. Before reaching out, do some research and check if the broker tends to handle all the asset classes we've mentioned, or if they specialize in one, such as office or retail. I always prefer having a specialist who knows a submarket and specific product. With generalists, the old saying usually applies: "Jack of all trades; master of none."

Attorneys

Just as all brokers aren't the same, attorneys come with many different specialties and areas of expertise. For real estate investments, it's of utmost importance to know professionals in the legal industry who transact in your market. Here are a few titles to help you become familiarized with these players.

Transactional Real Estate Attorney

When you move forward with a project, this kind of attorney will do your purchase and sale contracts. For both buying and selling, a transactional real estate attorney will usually work with the bank during the process. They'll be involved with the loan documents, title documents, and transfer documents. They'll also be present during the closing, which is the time when the loan process is finalized and the title moves from the seller to the buyer. A knowledgeable transactional real estate attorney should also be able to pull together your partnership agreements for you and your investors.

Landlord-Tenant Attorney

As a specialist in the laws surrounding landlord and tenant rights, this team member brings incredible value to various processes. Think of this type of attorney as having your back when you're working to understand the leases attached to a property. They'll help you do up-front work to see how the leases are structured and advise you of any potential pitfalls.

For instance, suppose you are looking at a residential building with apartments that are subject to rent regulation. There may be a set price that the leases cannot exceed and certain filings that must be completed with the city or state. In regions without rent regulation, the landlord-tenant attorney might show you that the rents do not need to be regulated and are priced at fair market value, meaning the rents can be set according to the market conditions. Maybe rents are going up in a neighborhood because a lot of people are moving to the city and want to live in that location. Perhaps they are dropping because the borough used to have some great perks like lovely green areas and sports fields, but these have been closed and developed into warehouses. A landlord-tenant attorney might even clue you in that the rents are currently priced at fair market value but will soon be regulated.

After you close on a property, you might lean on this team member again if issues arise with the tenants. Suppose you have a tenant that was in the place before you got the property and remains there after the sale. The tenant doesn't pay rent, and it eventually gets to the point where you have to go through an eviction process and ask them to leave. The landlord-tenant attorney again will swoop in to help you through these sometimes challenging eviction processes, which, I might add, are much easier to go through with someone else on your side, rather than doing it all on your own.

Tax Attorney

These professionals are experts in handling legal tax matters, and you can turn to them if you want to ask questions about taxes on your real estate transactions. There are often capital gains tax considerations when real estate is sold, meaning the profits from the sale could be subject to a certain tax rate. You could also consult this type of counsel when carrying out a 1031 exchange, which involves switching one investment property for another to defer capital gains taxes. (Read more about the 1031 exchange in Step 10.) There are qualified intermediaries that will need to be utilized during this process as well.

If you get a tax bill and feel that the amount is overstated, you can bring in a tax attorney to go over the details with you and offer advice. There are many kinds of tax advantages that can come with real estate investing that other investment vehicles don't offer. Therefore, working with a tax attorney is essential to sift through the different codes and fully realize that value. Bottom line: a great tax attorney will help you structure a transaction to make sure you are legally maximizing your tax benefits.

Land Use Attorney

If you're going to develop land or convert a building from one use to another, you'll want a strong land use attorney on your side. This professional will comb through the zoning laws associated with the property so you're aware of what can—and cannot—be done. They'll line up the building permits, oversee environmental matters, and review all the legalities related to the construction project. If there are cases that need to go to court, the land use attorney will present them before the judge.

Real Estate Accountants

You may know someone who works as a CPA or you might have hired one in the past to do your taxes. However, in real estate, accountants take on new meaning and play a distinct role. Think of the different money-related factors tied to a piece of property: you may need financial reports for the place that list out expenses and profits, spell out the revenue streams, or show the cash flow that is being generated. You'll also have to keep records of the transactions, rental information, lease records, and so on. It's best to have a professional involved in these steps to make sure everything is in order. After all, careful tracking of the finances will help you keep tabs on the property, and good business practices tell us that solid record keeping gives you a view of where you're at—and where you're going—especially in terms of a return. When forming your team, seek out an accountant that specializes in real estate and has worked with properties in the past that line up with your interests.

Architects

Suppose you're looking at a project in which you'd like to carry out some renovations. You can start to imagine and envision change as you walk through the property. Do you draw up the plans yourself? (Quick side note: The creativity factor is probably what I love most about real estate investments! There are so many ways to look at a property, and a myriad of nuances to draw on . . . it's a bit like moving puzzle pieces around to ultimately create a masterpiece. We'll dig into this more in Step 4.)

For the purpose of this discussion, we'll point out that it's best to have an expert come in and draw up a detailed plan of the project. An architect can also help you think through how space might be used, along with design trends and current market demand. Are renters looking for an ample kitchen with an island so they can cook at home? A tiny kitchen and larger living space because they tend to order in? A solid architect can help you take a floor plan and move it to the next level.

General Contractors

When carrying out renovations or other construction projects, you'll need the involvement of a general contractor. If you work with a reputable and experienced one, you can expect great quality and timely deliverables. They'll steer you through the project from the starting quote to the final walk-through. The best part? If the two of you build something together and it goes well, it can be the start of a long-term, valuable relationship. Just think, as you take on bigger projects, the contractor can move with you, which benefits everyone involved.

INSIDER TIP

Don't grab the first general contractor you meet. Ask someone you trust in the real estate space for a recommendation and review the contractor's past work before making a commitment. Ask if their previous project was on time and on budget.

Title Agents

You may be asking, "James, are we done yet?" Bear with me, because many of these players, including this one, play a small but vital role in the transaction. A title agent researches the title of the property. These professionals bring many benefits and reduce key risks related to a project. The word "title" in real estate refers to the right that a person or group possesses to legally own a piece of property. The title will list information about the property's boundaries and how it can be used. Obviously, it's a big deal to make sure you receive a legal title when you carry out a transaction for a piece of property. If you're coming in as a buyer, you want to know that you receive the correct title and legally own the space.

A title agent will look through real estate records in your area to make sure the property title is valid. They'll also investigate any unpaid expenses attached to the property, such as property taxes that weren't sent in or liens, which are legal rights for creditors to claim a property. A lien can come into play if an owner takes out a loan and puts up the property as collateral. If the owner stops repaying the loan, the lender could have the right to come in and take over the property. The lender can sell it to recoup their losses.

As you can see, there are a lot of things that can go wrong with a title. That's why title agents are key, and a good one will do more than the necessary research to make sure the title is on the up-and-up. They will also help you navigate getting insurance for the title. This coverage protects you once you become the new owner if any questions or disagreements about the title come up after the sale has taken place.

Owner's Representatives

You may not come across these individuals on your first projects, but they are worth mentioning here for the sake of covering all potential team members you could interact with throughout your real estate investing career. When you acquire very large projects, you might bring on an owner's representative, who is someone that—you guessed it—represents you as the owner. They will likely bring some layers of expertise in areas like construction, design, and architecture. The owner's representative might be present for various stages of the projects carried out on the property, from conceptual meetings early in the process to the completion of the construction. They will often help get permits for the work being done, make sure the project meets local requirements, hire contractors and other firms, and manage the project budget and schedule.

Following this line of thought, if you secure a large apartment building, you might want help overseeing its renovation. You could call on someone to represent you who has renovated many apartment buildings in the past. Perhaps you tell them, "Listen, I don't know about construction, and I need someone looking out for me." That person could help organize and carry out the renovations. You can sit down and talk to them about your goals for the project. Then, on your behalf, they will visit the site regularly and keep track of timelines. They'll help projects stay on schedule and update you regularly on the progress and completed milestones.

Property Managers

Last but certainly not least, we have the person who plays a hands-on role in the day-to-day management of the property. Suppose you buy a building, and you know that you don't have the time to interact with tenants, collect rents, or pay the bills. Not to worry—a property manager can oversee all these activities. You'll pay them for their services, and in light of our discussion on team players, I think it's fairly evident why you'll want a top-notch manager. If they stay organized and do a good job of handling daily operations, your investment has a better chance of performing well, leading to higher returns. Property managers for a building might be referred to as third-party managers or managing agents. I often partner with a managing agent on deals. I find the opportunity and the managing agent runs the properties.

When you're ready to go one step further with team building, check out the Bonus Step in this book. There, I share the tools and resources needed to create a dream team. It's a way to uplevel your long-term game in the real estate investing world.

KEY TAKEAWAYS

- To get a competitive return, you'll want to work with a high-performing team for every deal you make. Bringing the right players to the table in each transaction will help you gain an edge over other beginning real estate investors.

- A sponsor, or general partner, tends to oversee an entire investment from start to finish and handles the day-to-day asset management. Limited partners make investments and are not involved in the day-to-day but can have major decision-making rights such as when to sell or refinance; they oftentimes also put up the majority of the equity in the deal.

- For your first investment, you may benefit by partnering with an experienced sponsor who has the ability to execute the business plan and raise the equity and debt to close the deal. Even if you have to give up some of the economics, you'll begin developing your own track record, which will help you raise money for future opportunities.

- Investment sale brokers can help you identify properties that meet your interests and walk you through the purchasing process; they'll also be there when you're ready to sell later.

- Some of the other professionals you'll want in your contact list include mortgage brokers, attorneys, real estate accountants, architects, general contractors, title agents, and property managers.

STEP 3

Spot the Gems

When I was a young broker, and new to all things real estate related, I canvassed the neighborhoods in my area, going door-to-door to meet owners and investors and to learn about deals. Since I was new to the game, not everyone was eager to talk to me about their properties. A few, however, opened the door when I knocked and picked up the phone when I called.

During this time, one individual, Matt Blesso, who is the CEO and founder of Blesso Properties, noticed my hustling—and he took the time to talk to me. He asked if I would flip a contract he had signed for a property in the West Village. It was a mixed-use building, with an old restaurant on the ground floor and apartments above.

The original contract was for $2.2 million, which was a great deal. In real estate, if set up correctly, a potential buyer can essentially get a contract to acquire a property, and then sell the rights to another buyer. Since Matt had found such a low price, the idea was that another buyer would pay him a premium to get the contract. Matt could walk away with a profit, and the next buyer would get the property.

I took on the task. Within a few weeks, I received multiple offers for around $2.6 million. Thinking the flip would take place, I reasoned I would charge a commission for finding the offer. Then we would all move on.

As it turned out, Matt had another idea up his other sleeve. He approached me and brought up the thought of not flipping it at all. Instead, he had decided to go ahead with the purchase. When I heard this, I asked if I could invest as well. We could hold the contract, buy the place together as partners, and then renovate it. His business plan involved turning the current spaces into condos, and then selling them to homebuyers.

While negotiating the contract to purchase the place, Matt had spotted some ways to reduce the price further. He was able to get the contract down to $1.95 million. This was an incredible figure for the property. I came on as the first investor.

But before we could carry out the project, we needed to arrange financing to purchase the building and convert the spaces to residential condos. Matt and I found two others who were interested as well, making a total of four investors.

INSIDER TIP

The only thing you can't change about an investment is what you paid for it. Buy right!

We each put in an amount to start. I invested $150,000 and, together with the other partners, we put in $750,000 for the place and financed the rest. Then we dug in and oversaw the construction to turn the spaces into condos. Less than two years later, the condos were completed, and we sold them. Through the sale, we brought in a net profit of nearly $5 million. On a personal level, my investment had provided me with a return of 350% over only 1.8 years.

Now, you might be thinking, "Not bad," but the story gets better. You see, while we sold the condos, we initially kept the retail portion of the building. Later, after we sold the retail space, our profits grew even larger. We even sold the air rights from the building for an extra pop! The retail space had a sale price of $4.4 million, which was more than double the original price of the entire building.

We placed the profits into a multifamily unit investment in Brooklyn. Over time, Matt and I went on to invest in other deals as partners. While we've had many successes along the way, that first deal together will forever remain in my mind. Twenty years later, I've gotten all my money back from this investment many times over and am still receiving cash flow from the rental units. It's truly the gift that keeps on giving—and building greater returns.

While this might seem like a feat that can only be accomplished after spending decades in the real estate industry, I can assure you it doesn't have to be the case. That apartment building with Matt, which led to a great outcome for everyone involved, was my first New York City investment. I mention this because it shows that even as you start out, a solid find can bring you long-lasting benefits.

My story on that initial New York City investment highlights three important aspects of spotting a diamond in the rough: we need to understand the competitive landscape, we want to recognize the characteristics of a good opportunity, and we must know how to discover them. Tread correctly in these, and you'll increase your chances of reaping strong returns. In the following sections, I'll further explain each of these three concepts.

KNOW THE COMPETITIVE LANDSCAPE

When buying, it's essential to understand the details about how a property will be sold. For instance, is the property being widely marketed with a bid deadline? Would the owner consider a preemptive offer before going to market? Does the owner want an unsolicited offer?

Unlike residential, commercial listings are often underexposed to the market and sold without a listing broker. This can lead to buying opportunities where a property may be acquired for less than its true value. That said, not all off-market deals are bargains—they can also carry a lot more risk. Here are the various ways properties are typically sold, starting with the broadest market exposure and moving to the least exposed.

On Market

Exclusive right to sell. This means the seller has engaged a sales broker to run a full marketing process. If the broker is doing their job, they will inform their investor list, post the property on a variety of multiple listing services, and send the listing to the brokerage community. This should produce the widest exposure to generate the most competitive offers, leading to the highest price. Sellers take note!

The advantages of this method are that the broker will have taken the time to research and vet the property information and should be able to provide the right due diligence materials for the buyer. The seller's broker also "controls the deal," so they can advise the buyers of the bidding landscape.

I would also make the case that sometimes it takes a marketing process to educate a seller on the true market value. With this in mind, sometimes it's best to be the last buyer in as opposed to the first. Still, you'll be competing with the most buyers in this arrangement. You might go through multiple rounds of bids, have to do extensive due diligence, and spend legal dollars before you even know that you have a deal!

Exclusive agency. This is a variation of the exclusive right to sell setup. The seller has the ability to sell the property directly to their own buyers without having to compensate the listing broker. Here the broker is only compensated if they bring the ultimate buyer. Don't get any ideas of going straight to the seller if a broker brings you the listing. Always honor and "protect" the broker. If you don't, that broker (and their company) will probably never show you another deal. The listing agent should have the proper information and a good rapport with the seller. Unfortunately, the broker doesn't entirely control the deal; the seller might transact directly with one of their buyers to save a fee.

Auctions. These can range from sales on the courtroom steps to online platforms such as Ten-X. Real estate auctions are usually supported by a listing agent. Banks and distressed sellers often turn to auctions because they are quick and happen on a defined timetable. Many of these sales are also mandated by the courts. However, auctions are widely publicized and can draw a large audience of sophisticated buyers who are well capitalized. You will need to get preapproved by the auction house and in many cases post a 10% deposit that would go hard (meaning the money is taken from you and may not be returned, depending on the terms for the deal) if you win the bid.

INSIDER TIP

At an auction, the seller may merely be looking to see how much a property could bring in; they might put the threshold high and then observe what buyers bid. Go prepared and keep within your comfort zone in terms of risk when naming your price. Stay disciplined with your pricing.

Because these properties are sold "as is, where is" on a quick timeline, you might have to rush your due diligence process. It is really difficult for the broker to give indicative pricing, as they won't know until auction day who shows up and where the bids shake out. Further, the auction platform may not reveal what the reserve price is, so the deal might not even trade unless it hits a minimum threshold.

Off Market

Buyer specific representation. Here a broker will get recognized by the seller to bring a specific buyer. In some cases, the owner won't even acknowledge the broker, so you will have to pay your broker to represent you. On the positive side, you likely won't be competing with multiple bidders. Your buyer broker will be advocating for you to get the best price. That said, there is no fiduciary with the seller and your broker. In fact, they are on different sides of the negotiating table. Don't expect the seller to show you their cards.

In some listing situations, having a broker represent you on the buy side can be a disadvantage. It means the seller's broker will have to split a fee. It's not the fiduciary thing to do, but listing brokers will sometimes give preference to their direct buyer so they get paid the full fee.

In any of these cases, the commission can be paid by the seller, buyer, or both. The key is disclosure. If you are going to pay a buyer broker to represent you, they need to disclose this to the seller. The broker should know this from their state licensing exams, but you don't want to get caught in the middle.

For sale by owner. Referred to as FSBOs in the residential world, some owners look to sell the property on their own. They might not even offer a fee to brokers in attempt to save paying a commission. This can be penny-wise and pound-foolish, but some owners think they know it all. While you might not have a lot of competition when buying directly from an owner, you'll also miss out on the advantages that come with a broker. Having a broker can help buyers and sellers find a middle ground. The seller might be unreasonable on their own regarding terms or conditions.

WHAT MAKES A PROPERTY A GREAT BUY

Let's say you're looking online at some properties and trying to decipher on which one to make an offer. You head to a broker's website and compare two listings. Now, which one is the better deal? Are both of them great buys? Or neither one?

If you follow a precise set of guidelines when perusing opportunities, it will be easier to see where your attention—and funds—should go. Here are the top characteristics I look for that can help the winners rise to the top of my bidding list.

1. A Motivated Seller

Why did the seller put the property up for sale? This question may seem like an obvious one to ask, but you'd be very surprised how few buyers actually pose it. When you inquire about the reason behind a sale, the answer can reveal a lot about the property and the price you'll pay for it.

If you learn that a sale is taking place because of a negative financial situation, it could mean the property might be a great deal. Good buys often come as a result of a bankruptcy, partnership dispute, or financial distress. In my experience, estate sales frequently mean a lower price. The owners are typically adult children who inherit the property and are eager to get it off their hands, deal with the taxes involved, and move on.

In 2020, I brokered an estate sale in the heart of Greenwich Village. Pre-pandemic, the property, which consisted of a restaurant and about 72 apartments above it, was valued at about $32 million.

Over the course of 60 days, coinciding with the onset of Covid-19, the price plummeted. The buyer who stayed on ultimately got the place for $22.5 million—an incredible deal!

Remember, this was an estate sale. A discretionary seller would never have dropped their price by $10 million in 60 days. In this case, however, the sellers were motivated to get the property off their hands, which generated an ideal opportunity for the buyer.

2. Lack of Marketing Exposure

Sometimes an owner doesn't want to work with a broker to sell their property. The reasons for this can vary: maybe they would rather not pay a broker's fee, or perhaps they don't want the tenants to know about the sale. Whatever the reason, this can also mean that the owner doesn't receive as many offers. They may be unaware of what price they could ultimately get.

Early on in my career, I found an advertisement in a print publication listing a property that was "For Sale by Owner." Now, listing a property for sale in the paper might seem like a great way to gain exposure. In reality, however, most investors rarely look through these listings. Instead, they wait for their brokers to present them with opportunities.

I didn't want to be like every other investor, so I searched places like the newspaper listings to see what was there. After viewing the property, I thought it was a great opportunity, as the price was lower than it likely would have been if a broker had been involved in selling the building. I partnered with another buyer and got the place for under $1 million. We then sold the property again within 24 months for over four times the amount we initially paid!

On some occasions, you'll find a broker mismatch in the listings. By this I mean a broker might take on a property that is outside of their area of expertise. A residential broker listing an office property, for instance, may not know the best price and terms to include for the property. You'll likely be up against less competition if the broker is unable to fully expose the property to the market. They might end up underpricing the asset as well.

To find properties that aren't well marketed, create your own treasure hunt. Write letters to owners of buildings, asking if they'd like to sell. Strike up a conversation with superintendents about the property they're overseeing and if a sale could happen in the near future. If you see a sign listing the property as available for leasing, call up the number and see if they'll consider selling.

INSIDER TIP

Don't wait for deals to come to you. Look for opportunities in places that others don't bother to pursue.

---

3. Neglected Property

Owners don't always keep a sharp eye on their properties. They might, for instance, purchase a multifamily building and have someone else run it for them. I know of a case in New York City in which the owner of a 30-unit apartment building in Chelsea didn't live anywhere near the place. He resided in Florida and let the superintendent manage the place. The super did uphold his managing duties, and probably enjoyed doing it, too, but the fact was that some of the tenants were taking advantage of the situation.

Their rents were regulated, meaning they couldn't be raised past a certain point. With little supervision, the residents of the building moved out of their places and sublet them (think "Airbnbing" them) at a higher price than what they were paying in rent. This allowed the tenants to make some income off of property they didn't own. Unfortunately, it wasn't legal for them to do so. When a buyer swooped in, he was able to clean out the illegal tenants, charge higher rents, and increase the building's profitability through better management.

4. Repositioning Opportunity

When you look at a place, how do you see it? Do you take it in as it is, or do you imagine the way it *could* be? Having a vision, a bit of creativity, and a knowledge base that is aware of changes that could be made can pack a big punch. For instance, could a seven-unit family building be renovated and turned into a single-family home? If so, what would the return be?

Looking at a property with an eye of what it could become can be the ticket to a big future sales price. In the example at the beginning of this chapter, I shared how three investors and myself reimagined a building's space by turning it into condos and then selling them. This concept is called repositioning and refers to changing a property so that it serves a different purpose—and frequently results in generating more revenue. (We'll look more at value-add opportunities in Step 8.)

5. A Neighborhood Ready to Pop

Let's say you and I are watching the evening news together. The camera turns to reveal a reporter standing in the Bronx, in a spot where a new subway station is set to open. If we view that news piece through the scope of a real estate investor, we see much more than a new metro stop being added to an old neighborhood. I might talk to you about the impact that new station will make in terms of buildings, values, and opportunities. We could then turn off the news and start sifting through property listings right around that upcoming station.

Neighborhoods that change for the better mean higher values and increased returns. The trick, of course, is to discover them *before* everyone else. Not to worry, I have tools for that too: follow trends, get on a community board to find out what's happening, watch the local news, and look at what real estate pioneers are doing.

If you see art gallery owners buying up buildings for next to nothing in a predominantly industrial part of town, that could be a sign to jump in and bid. Once the art galleries are up, everything else slides into place: retail shops, restaurants, apartments . . . you name it, it will be there, and it will be worth much more than you pay today. And remember, there is no substitute for walking through areas to spot trends yourself. Stroll down streets and watch for construction projects underway; ask servers at the local café about what's changing; imagine ways you could reinvent the landscape of the neighborhood through a real estate project of your own.

6. Zoning Changes

New York City's zoning regulations are incredibly complex, making it tough to sort through the rules of what you can—and cannot—do to a property. In other places, you might find a different system (or fewer pages on zoning), but one thing remains the same: when a shift occurs, opportunity abounds. It could mean the difference between being able to build in a place where you couldn't before and the chance to put in a new type of property, or to change an existing property into a revenue-producing one . . . the potential here is huge.

Several years ago, there was an area along Sixth Avenue in Chelsea that focused on manufacturing and had regular flea markets up and down the street. The overseeing board for the strip looked at it and realized this section was in the heart of Manhattan, above subway lines, and offered virtually no residential spaces. The board decided to allow property owners to build residential towers of up to 30 or 40 stories. In a matter of years, the whole quarter shot up.

Think of the potential there for investors of all sizes. Even if you weren't going to build a tower of 30 or 40 stories, you could have purchased a smaller building and still benefited from the change to a residential zone.

7. Finding Value Where Others Do Not

I know of a developer who purchased an old switching station that had a lot of mechanical space for about $25 million. Then he carried out a particularly genius move. He discovered a zoning loophole that allowed him to create residential space on the property by using mechanical deductions. He developed additional floors and eventually sold luxury condos, with a sellout of over $1 *billion*.

8. Properties with Increased Rent Potential

In some markets, you could find a retailer or residential tenant paying a low rent that the government has set for them. This is called rent regulation, as I've mentioned; it is also sometimes referred to as rent control. It basically means that certain rights are given to renters in terms of the amount they pay. For instance, tenants may be entitled to pay no more than $800 a month, regardless of how rent prices are trending. Other newcomers might have to pay double that amount or more in hot markets.

I've observed cases in which investors take on a property and buy out the tenants. This means to give tenants an incentive like a cash payout to leave the property. Then the investors increase the rent. The next wave of tenants pays more in rent, which increases the profitability of the place. If you're going to consider doing this, make sure you are working with a landlord-tenant attorney to determine if you can, in fact, increase an apartment's rent to the market rate.

In some places, vacation properties can unlock an excellent development opportunity with significant increased rent potential. I have owned vacation homes in Cape Cod that I rent out for almost the entire tourist season. You could buy a lot and build a home in an up-and-coming resort area, with the goal of renting it out to incoming waves of vacationers. Or you might get a place currently designed for one family and divide it into several units, each of which can then be rented out to travelers. You could even take a vacation home that attracts travelers with midsized budgets and add features so that it draws in vacationers seeking luxurious accommodations. This, too, can lead to a rent increase and greater return over time.

The lesson here lies in thinking outside the box. It encompasses taking fresh eyes to absorb a place others might view as tired, old, or only slightly profitable. This is your chance to be creative, to get excited about the possibilities, and to take action to make it happen.

UNDERSTANDING SALES PRICE

When you look for properties, you'll often come across references to price per square foot (PPSF). This is a term that is used to describe the value of a building. It is calculated by dividing the total sales price by the number of square feet in a building. It can be applied to apartment buildings, offices, retail, or any type of property.

This figure is helpful when you're comparing different options. You might see a 40,000 square foot property that is selling for $250 a square foot, making it a $10 million property. Then you look at a 30,000-square-foot property of the same asset class selling for $500 a square foot, or $15,000,000. Which one is the better deal? Consider the PPSF as a starting point. You can ask questions to see why one property has a higher PPSF than the other. Is it in better condition? Is it in a nicer location? Is the cheaper property encumbered by a tenant paying a below market rent? Is the more expensive property simply overpriced?

After starting with the PPSF, find out the tenancy, condition of the building, and price per unit. (This is found by dividing the sales price by the number of units, or apartments). Also look for the capitalization rate. Often called the cap rate, this term refers to the rate of return an investment will provide and it's frequently included in the listing details. (We'll look more at cap rate in Step 5.) You can also check the price per unit, which is another metric used to compare properties.

Do your research. There are great data-providing services available to look at comparable sales too, like Reonomy. Look for eblasts, which will cover sales information. Sales brokers send out quarterly reports, so get on their mailing lists. Instagram and Twitter will likely have handles from your area that list great data about recent sales. Traded (traded.co) is a great resource I follow. You can even call the listing broker for a property and ask about comparable sales.

GET TO KNOW YOUR BROKERS

Over the years, I have realized that working with the right investment sales broker can make a world of difference. These individuals represent real estate investors who want to buy, sell, or finance property. Investment sales brokers typically offer strategic advice and have inside knowledge of what's going on in the market. Furthermore, they have access to incredible deals.

Given these capabilities, investment sales brokers are an essential participant in real estate investments. According to Beau Berry, who wrote *Multifamily Brokers Who Dominate*, 92.5% of deals in his Florida market are brokered. Even if this percentage is lower in other markets, brokers still handle the majority of sales. Given this, it is essential to form strong bonds with them to become one of their first calls for new opportunities. You'll often work with multiple brokers. You might be able to see some properties on their website, but that broker might have additional places that are not listed. By developing a relationship, you can increase the odds of learning about these hidden deals and finding options that are not online.

Through my experience, I've developed tactics to make the most of your relationship with investment sales brokers. Here is a list of tips I suggest:

- **Routinely connect.** When you're a newcomer, this might be a bit of a challenge, as most brokers like to transact only with repeat clients. That means you have to be that much more persistent. Do not wait for brokers to call you. Offer to meet them for coffee. Then call them at least once a month to follow up.
- **Make sure it is not a one-way street.** Give brokers tips for deals that you know about but are not going to pursue.
- **Show dedication.** Demonstrate that you are committed. Have the right partners to move quickly and be able to close.
- **Send them your deal criteria.** Share a list of what you're looking for in an acquisition with brokers so they know what you're interested in. If they come across a property that fits your criteria, chances are they'll reach out to you.
- **Offer early.** When the deal is right, offer to preempt the property before it goes to market. This involves making an offer before the date that the seller designates to start accepting bids.
- **Dig deeper.** When you talk to a broker, always ask, "What's in your pipeline?" You want to know what deals they are working on which have not yet hit the market.
- **Let others go ahead.** Sometimes, it's best to be the last buyer in a deal. This is especially true when the seller's situation changes over time.

- **Be creative.** Harry Helmsley, a real estate billionaire, was known for saying, "Your price. My terms." Work with brokers to find out what the most important terms are in the deal.
- **Follow them online.** Ask to get on an email list and follow brokers on social media. You might find a great sale through a broker's Instagram post.

In addition to working in a smart way with investment sales brokers, finding that perfect deal often involves heading out on your own. I've seen that properties sold directly from the owner are sometimes the perfect investment in terms of price and return. The best ones are usually not even listed on the market yet.

Given these tendencies, it can be valuable to seek out owners who are selling property and ask for information. Discovering them, of course, is not easy. Here are my suggestions for finding off-market opportunities that are sold by the owner:

- **Reach out.** Never be afraid to contact the owner directly. If you see a vacant building, call the owner. Ownership is publicly available in most cities or made readily available from private services like Reonomy.
- **Mention the perks.** When you speak to the owner, bring up the benefits of selling off-market and not going through a long process. These advantages include not bothering the tenants and not having to pay a broker's fee.
- **Grab a pen.** Don't hesitate to write a letter to the owner, expressing your interest.
- **Talk to others.** Speak to the supers on the block of the property you're interested in. They often know their neighbors, especially the ones who might be hard to find online.
- **Participate publicly.** Get involved in the neighborhoods where you want to invest. Community board meetings can be a good place to find owners and hear their plans.

- **Look for abandoned projects.** Research their lenders and call them!
- **Follow up on disappearances.** Track listings that were on the market and came off. Sometimes it takes a seller a few marketing attempts to become more realistic.

INSIDER TIP

Look for poorly marketed properties. These "listings" will rarely be posted on multiple listing sites. There might just be a "For Sale" sign hung outside or a mention on a broker's website.

I'll never forget meeting Matt, making that initial investment of $150,000, and reaping the benefits from the deal. At the time, it was an exciting and thrilling process and one that spurred me on to find other properties. Along the way, I learned many lessons and honed some smart strategies to spot those truly incredible deals.

Use the checklists and tips in this chapter to guide the discussions you have with brokers, and to do some undercover work in the off-market realm. With some practice, you'll be able to find a deal of your own. The beauty of real estate investing is that rewards tend to shower on those who seek them. The jewel of a property you snag could bring you significant returns, and those returns could keep coming, year after year.

KEY TAKEAWAYS

- Properties are sold in a variety of ways, ranging from on market to off market and with varying degrees of exposure and risk.

- Certain characteristics can help you sort out great buys as you search, including a motivated seller, lack of marketing exposure, neglected property, repositioning opportunities, neighborhoods ready to pop, zoning changes, your ability to find value where others do not, and properties with increased rent potential.

- Use the price per square foot (PPSF) to compare properties and research details to better understand each one. Other metrics for comparison include capitalization rates and price per unit.

- Build relationships and stay in regular touch with brokers to source opportunities. That said, don't be afraid to also reach out directly to owners to find deals on your own.

STEP 4

Know What to Look For

Here's a crazy-but-true story: I've sold a building that collapsed right before closing. At one time, that building existed, standing up, right across the street from where my wife and I lived.

When the seller came to me and asked for help putting it up for sale, I went to take a look. The property was a façade and nothing more. The shaky front wall of the building was actually propped up . . . and there was nothing behind it! To my amazement, people wanted to come see the front of the building, as they were interested in possibly purchasing the property. I would take them to the place, open the door, and voila: there was nothing beyond it.

An engineer came to have a look and give an assessment of the property. I met him there, and following my usual routine, I opened the door of the front panel. When he saw that there was a door—and no more—he ran in the opposite direction. Then he told me, "This building—or actually, this façade—is going to come down at any moment."

Turns out, the engineer was right. We found a buyer for the place, and a week before closing, my wife called me. "You're not going to believe this," she said, "but they just closed the street because the building collapsed."

The good fortune of this tale is that no one was near the front when it fell, and no one was hurt. The street shut down so the remains could be cleared, and I went on—believe it or not—to sell that place.

That story (and trust me, I have a lot of crazy tales!) only emphasizes the fact that properties can come in many shapes and forms. They might look a lot different when you tour them in person than how they sound when an owner first tells you about them or how they appear on Instagram. In addition to understanding the asset classes of real estate and building your team, you'll want to tour a place before you make a bid.

At first glance, the concept of a walkthrough might seem like basic knowledge. You may be asking, "Shouldn't we just go and look at the property? Isn't that what's typically done in real estate, regardless of whether the space is a home or office or retail space?"

I see a property tour as a critical step in the real estate investment process. It's much more than making sure the building won't collapse, or at least knowing it will, as some buyers may want to demolish the structure and start from the ground up. Herein lies your chance to see the opportunities that can be leveraged. It's an "on-the-ground" way to glean inside knowledge about the place and discover how value can be added.

A great walkthrough can lead to renovations that help the property generate more income and produce long-term returns. It could also help you find ways to make a few big changes and then sell the place for a higher price. I have done thousands of walkthroughs and witnessed, firsthand, what amazing finds happen during this process.

For the purpose of this chapter, let's differentiate virtual tours from in-person showings. In today's virtual world, it's easier than ever to see a place from afar. Perhaps you live in San Diego and are planning a move to Chicago. You could a look at images and videos of two-bedroom condos in Chicago on your device while you sit on the couch of your California living room. Besides, if you're house shopping for a place in the Windy City during January, chances are you're more than happy to tour it virtually from miles away, in the land of sun and warmth.

Keep in mind that what you see online isn't always a true reflection of the place and neighborhood. That leaning façade of a building I sold may have looked pretty good from a certain street angle (before it fell). If I, as a broker, didn't clue you in about the realities of the building (or in this case, the lack thereof), and you bought the property without stepping foot into it, you would have been in for a big surprise. There are also the components we've mentioned in earlier chapters, including the insight you'll gain from walking a neighborhood and seeing what the other properties in the area are like.

To understand how to carry out a walkthrough in a way that unveils value, let's begin by examining how it compares to touring residential, or single-home, properties. We'll also discuss who we should bring along on a walkthrough. We'll look at what questions to ask, how to find value, and where to spot red flags.

INSIDER TIP

Don't accept the way a property is currently being presented; look for ways to reimagine the space to increase its value.

TOURING RESIDENTIAL AND INVESTMENT PROPERTIES

There are some similarities between walking through a home you want to buy and looking at an office building for sale. During both tours, you're interested in looking at the overall condition of the place and are likely thinking about how you can improve it. You'll also be going over costs for those changes, either in your head or with others who are on the tour.

When you look at a residential space, there are typically some fail-safe measures in place designed to reduce your risk as a buyer. For instance, you can look at the property disclosure form, in which the owner provides detailed information about the condition of the home. Thanks to this documentation, you'll see records of repairs that have been done on the place, any insurance claims that have been made, and other potentially major issues, like a roof that leaks—all before you sign!

In addition, the federal government requires certain disclosures to be made, including if there is lead-based paint on the property or other hazards like the presence of asbestos, which can cause cancer and related health problems. States and counties also have laws regarding what must be disclosed for residential real estate. Some states require that if a death or murder occurs on the property, that fact has to be shared with the new potential homeowners. Others ask for disclosures related to sex offenders who live nearby.[1]

Then there's the professional home inspector who comes on to the scene. They'll carefully survey the residence, reviewing both the inside and the outside. The inspector will check the foundation, the condition of the roof, the air conditioning and heating system, the plumbing, the electrical system, and so on. Thanks to this thorough inspection, you again get a better sense of exactly what you are buying. If the inspector finds the foundation has a large crack, you can look at how much it will cost to fix it—along with your other options for dealing with the issue.

After some of these initial steps, the negotiation can begin. Perhaps you look at a home that's listed on the market for $500,000. After you tour it yourself and get a report from the inspector, you see that the roof needs to be replaced. You might approach the seller and explain that you're interested in the home but noticed that you'll have to put in a new roof. If you see other repairs to be made, you'll bring those to the negotiating table, too. The bids can go back and forth between you and the seller as you work to find a price with which you are both comfortable, and terms you can agree on regarding the sale of the place.

You may be familiar with the residential give-and-take that goes on when buying a home. In the real estate investing world, some of those measures don't carry over. If you're an investor, you're considered to be a professional. As such, you'll be expected to do your own due diligence. You'll need to investigate the place to see what condition it is in, how its financials stand, and how much it is worth. (The initial due diligence starts during the walkthrough; we'll dive into its later stages in Step 7.)

In most cases, in my experience, investment properties are sold "as is." This means they come to the buyer with their defects, whether they are known or unknown. The place could be in great or not-so-great condition. Sometimes that will be obvious, like the example I shared of the toppling building. Prospective buyers who came on the property told me, "James, this looks like it could fall at any minute." And it did. (Turns out, their due diligence was correct!) Other times, it isn't as straightforward to see the real condition of a property.

Part of the reason for this lies in the fact that investment properties are subject to different requirements than residential properties, including what I mentioned regarding the property disclosure forms and inspections, which are a legal must with residences but not always mandated by law in the real estate investment space. (That said, certain disclosures are required for investment property, such as notifying if there is lead paint in a building.)

Another factor involves the size of the place. While you can typically tour a home—even a large residence—and see every room (or close to it), that's not always the case with real estate investment property. If you go to a 30-unit apartment building, don't expect to see all the closets, every kitchen, and all the bedrooms inside every unit. Instead, you'll see a sampling of the spaces to get a representative idea of the property. Perhaps in a 30-unit apartment, the owner tells you that half of the units have been renovated. The two of you walk through one or two of the apartments that have been remodeled to see what they are like. Then you tour one or two of the units that haven't been renovated. Once you've seen those, you can carry on with steps of lining up your own inspection of the place.

BRINGING ALONG YOUR TEAM

With a nod to Step 2, in which we laid out the key players you'll need on your team, here is a chance to see those folks in action. When touring a property, there is no exact list of people who should come along. It will depend on what type of asset class you are viewing, who your partner (or partners) is in the deal, and the size and potential of the space. Rather than ending with those vague statements, I'll break down some examples to help you start thinking about who might give the place a look—and when to bring them.

Let's say you spot a six-family apartment building that is advertised as needing to be renovated. When you research the rents the tenants are paying, along with what the tenants in the building across the street are paying, you see the rents on the other side of the street are much higher than the ones in the building for sale. Since the listing announces there is work to be done, you'll want someone on that first tour to come along and evaluate what renovations should be carried out. In this case, you might call on a residential leasing broker (and if you have one in your contacts already, excellent! If not, now's the time to ask a trusted partner or broker for a referral).

Here's how the leasing broker can help you reimagine the place. Rather than giving you a long list of options regarding what you could do, the leasing broker will come into the tour with inside knowledge on how the market is performing. Where is the demand? What are renters in the area looking for? Maybe they'll suggest that you add granite counter tops, stainless steel appliances and dishwashers in the kitchen, put in a new glass shower stall in the bathroom, paint, redo the floors, and leave the rest. Or they could suggest improvements like Amazon lockers in the entryway, so that households that order goods to be delivered don't have to make sure they are home when the packages arrive. A roof deck or bike storage might be other ways to add value.

If you're considering a newly built office property, the same concept holds true. You could bring in an office leasing broker who specializes in landlord representation, which is known as "agency work." You might ask them questions such as, "What are the expectations for procuring a tenant? Should it just be a white box?" Maybe the leasing broker will recommend building out partitions as well as glass conference rooms. Or they may encourage you to deliver the space "turnkey," such as a ready-to-go space with a kitchen and bathrooms built out.

Across all asset classes, when you consider doing some significant work, you might want to bring in an architect and a general contractor. They'll help you sort through questions surrounding where an additional wall could be placed, or if it is practical to create a more open floor plan. An engineer will give a structural perspective on how a place could practically be reworked, too, such as if it's possible to switch around the bedroom and bathroom, move the kitchen to a different area, and so on. You can expect them to look at where the beams are and help you review major issues, such as a sagging floor or cracked walls.

These players will help you see where your limitations are, while simultaneously helping you to avoid overextending the project. For instance, drawing on the apartment building example in which renovations need to be carried out, a leasing broker can point out additions that really aren't worthwhile. Maybe they'll say that no one in the neighborhood uses their roof deck, so it's not considered a top feature. Or they'll recommend that the two-bedroom units remain that way, as there's no need to make the place into a high-end one-bedroom, given that renters aren't jumping at these arrangements. They might advise against a complete build in an office space and assure you that companies prefer to customize it themselves.

Their suggestions can show you how to be what I call "best in class," which refers to offering a great deal for the market conditions. In other words, you don't want to provide upscale when there is no demand for it. You want to observe what comparable spaces have, make sure yours meets those expectations—or better yet, exceeds them—without going over the top. In the case of the apartment building that needs renovating, the upgrades you make, based on the leasing broker's advice, could bump up the rents so they're the same, or slightly more, than the units across the street.

You might tour a place once before making an offer . . . or you could walk through it two times, even a third, or more. The scope of the project you have in mind will play a big role in these decisions. Before reaching out to any team players, consider where you are in the process. For instance, you might do an initial tour with a leasing broker if you're thinking of renovating. Then you could go back with an architect or general contractor. You don't have to operate on the extreme side of bringing your entire team along on every walk-through, especially if there are multiple tours. I am always mindful of everyone's time. While an architect that you know might readily agree to see a place you want to redo, that same architect could get weary if you call them 20 times in one month to see different places several times.

It may seem contradictory, but for smaller assets, such as a duplex or triplex, it's almost always more important to bring a team on the tour. Here's why: every repair in a smaller property could have a greater impact on the bottom line of the investment. Suppose you go ahead and get the triplex you've toured and thought was in great condition, only to learn once you're the owner that the boiler needs to be replaced. That could wipe out your profit for half a year! You'll have to pay for a new boiler and its installment, while collecting rent from three tenants (or two, if you live in one of the units). There's more at stake with every repair.

On the other hand, if you have a team member along with you who knows what to check, they might help you reveal the boiler issue before any transaction has been made. Then you're suddenly in a better position. You can negotiate a lower price based on the repair that has to be made, or ask the seller for other concessions to make up for the boiler replacement you'll have to oversee. Remember that we said much of the due diligence is on you, and you'll notice a loss more in a smaller place with fewer rents than a larger place with 20 tenants. With higher levels of income coming in, the revenue could help lessen the impact you feel from the repairs that are being made.

RED FLAGS ON A PROPERTY

Here's another wild-but-true tale: Once on a tour in which I was showing a potential buyer a multifamily property, we ran into a hostile squatter tenant. He was standing in his doorway wearing a sleeveless shirt and a jeff cap (a "jeff cap" is also sometimes called a "flat cap" or "driving cap"). In his hands he held a crowbar. The buyer certainly didn't assume that person was going to leave easily!

Knowing what to look for on a property includes recognizing warning signs that the place might have significant problems. Sometimes your eye can catch more serious issues that need to be checked out, ranging from cracks in the walls to warped floors and water stains in the ceiling that signal a leak. These flags tend to cover structural issues and environmental concerns. There also could be indicators that the project simply isn't a good fit for your situation, such as a substantial renovation when you're looking for a core investment property that doesn't require much, or hardly any, work on your part.

Structural Issues

I promise this will be my last zany-but-true story for this chapter. I got stuck inside the elevator of a vacant building. It all started when

I was showing the property and along with several others entered the elevator. The lift started moving from one floor to the next . . . and then it stopped. Our phones didn't have a signal within the confines of the elevator. For several moments, I wondered how we were going to get out.

Then we spotted a trap door above. We worked to pry open the door and eventually got it to lift a crack. We removed it and were able to get out of the elevator and to safety. Every time I think of that incident, I recall being glad to get out! It's a good thing there was that trap door and we saw it; otherwise, I'm not sure if I would be here today to share the story with you.

Now, if you tour a building and the elevator doesn't work, perhaps a repair can be made. However, if there are signs that something is off with the structure (maybe the building is sinking!), you'll want to investigate. As I mentioned, properties for investments usually come "as is," so you will have to deal with major overhauls if they are needed once your name is attached to the title.

Environmental Concerns

Companies that use a variety of substances in their manufacturing plants run the risk of polluting the soil and violating environmental regulations. Auto repair shops also pose a threat, due to the oil they're using and the parts that are moving through. Same with cleaning companies that use heavy chemicals on-site for their processes. If it's not clear in the listing, during the walkthrough you'll be able to see and ask about the operations carried out in the place.

When it comes to environmental phases, there are generally three levels of inspection. Most lenders will require a Phase 1 inspection to be completed, which consists of researching the history of the property to see if there are any publicly revealed issues. There may also be an additional level of diligence needed, which is known as a Phase 2 inspection. In this case, soil samples will be drawn (if the seller allows—in some cases, they can refuse to have this done[2]). Taking samples will involve boring into the ground and evaluating the earth to determine if the dirt is free of contaminants; if it's not, there will usually be a remediation plan created to solve those problems. This remediation process is known as the Phase 3 inspection and is carried out after Phases 1 and 2 have been completed.[3]

Project Intensity

Suppose you find a partner and the two of you want to buy a duplex, fix it up, and rent out both spaces as a starting project. You see an ad for a two-story duplex with a basement that looks like it might be exactly what you have in mind. When you visit the property, you tour the upper levels, and they look like they could use some improvements. No problem, you think. Then you head to the basement. There are signs of water damage; when you investigate further, you learn that the place is located near a river and has had flooding issues in the past. An inspection reveals signs of mold infestation.

Now what do you do? Is this the fixer-upper you envisioned? Well, improvements are certainly in order, but maybe you and your partner were thinking of getting a place, spending three months to get it tenant ready, and then leasing it. If you go with this option, your timeline might be greatly extended. Will you have to replace some of the structure? Do those types of changes work for both of you from a financial perspective? Perhaps. Or maybe you both agree to walk away from this project and look for another option that doesn't come with so many to-dos.

One final caveat here: a run-down property doesn't have to drive buyers away. I've seen instances where a dilapidated building was just what the investor was hoping to get. In these cases, the buyer often wants to tear down the place and start over. Again, it's a matter of lining up the type of project with the amount of time and resources you want to invest.

> ## INSIDER TIP
>
> A red flag for one investor might be a golden opportunity for another investor.

RULES OF ENGAGEMENT

There is a certain level of risk associated with the walkthrough, especially because you are responsible for vetting the place and, as we've seen from my real-life examples, you can never be exactly sure of what you'll find. Collapsed façades, tenant run-ins, and broken elevators can—and do—happen. That said, you could go through buildings for the next 10 years and never have an incident (as perhaps makes sense since realtors and brokers are not considered to be high-risk jobs in terms of safety).

Still, there are some best practices I can share to help you avoid blunders during the property tour. These help you gain the upper edge over others in the market. They include taking on another perspective, knowing where to talk, and what conversations to have.

Become the Tenant

Before stepping inside a property, consider touring the area on foot. Walk the neighborhood and see what other buildings are on the market. If you're interested in a multifamily property that has places renting for $2,500, and notice that two blocks down, another multifamily property is listing places for $4,500, it's in your best interest to go have a look. Ask to see the listings of competitors, and go tour them, paying careful attention during the showings. You might notice attention called to a washer and dryer and learn that they are considered to be premium features for the area. Or you could observe that other buildings in the neighborhood have a bike room because a lot of tenants like to commute on two wheels.

Once you've visited comparable buildings in the neighborhood, go through the property you're interested in seeing. You can use your research to compare the places. In the case of a $2,500 versus $4,500 place, you'll be able to note differences and evaluate if you want to make improvements and then increase rents. This exercise will also help you avoid the risk of over-improving and charging rents that are too high for the area. If you make extensive changes to the $2,500/month per unit place and need to raise rents to $6,000 to cover the remodeling expenses, there might not be a market for it. Perhaps tenants will be happier in the $4,500/month places, which aren't quite as luxurious but are listed at a more comfortable price range for them.

INSIDER TIP

Know the competition in the market. If you're looking to reposition an apartment building, do you know how many available apartments are in the area? Do you know how long it will take to lease and the concessions required to secure a tenant?

Talk Away from the Tenants

It's a great idea to have a conversation with an owner or superintendent about the building when you carry out a tour. If there are tenants around, however, you'll want to save your questions for later. An unspoken rule in the walkthrough is that you don't interact with the tenants. In some cases, the owner might be selling the building and doesn't want the tenants to know the title will be changing hands. By avoiding the topic, you're respecting the owner's wishes. Also, the tenants may have questions about rent, and you usually don't want to address those until you've moved further along in the purchasing process.

In my experience, some of the best discussions with the owner take place on the roof of a building or in the boiler room. If it's a beautiful day, we might linger on the roof, where we can speak openly without fear of being overheard by tenants. During cold, wintry days, we'll likely be in the boiler room, which also offers a removed setting where open chatting can take place.

Put Criticism Aside

The way you approach these conversations with an owner during a walkthrough can enable you to learn crucial details about the place. Given this, when you bring up a topic, I always suggest starting with something positive. If you immediately point out flaws or mention a structural issue you're concerned about, the owner might clam up. Then it will be harder to get information that could help you learn more about how much to offer, what to do with the building, and other tidbits that will ultimately impact your return.

If the building is in a great location, you might start by pointing out that feature. Or you could ask how long the owner has had the building, and what initially drew them to the place. Once the conversation gets off to a good start, you may have the chance to ask why the owner is selling. This is a key question because it delves into the motivation behind the sale, which we touched on in Step 3.

You might get an answer such as this: "We've had a great run with this apartment building. Our family has owned it for 15 years and we even lived in one of the units when our kids were small. Now, the children are older, and it's just gotten to be too much work. We're looking to pass it on to someone else who is better able to commit the time needed to manage it." Maybe the conversation continues, and you learn that while the owner is happy with the income the place generates, they want to shift their investments to something else.

In other instances, you might find out the owner wants to cash out. Perhaps they need the funds to get them through something unexpected in their life, like having to retire early for health reasons. Or they might want to sell and reinvest in a different asset class, like moving from a multifamily property to an industrial site.

There are a myriad of reasons, but they all serve as clues for you to soak in and use as you evaluate the deal and move forward. If the owner is looking for cash and wants to sell fast, maybe they'll be open to a lower bid. If they're interested in reinvesting the funds but need time to find a new place, you could offer them a flexible timeline for closing. Oftentimes sellers that want to carry out a 1031 exchange have to identify the replacement properties, or the new places in which they will invest, within the first 45 days after the sale of the first property.[4] (More on this in Step 10.) In these situations, you can explain that you understand these time constraints. You might suggest being open to waiting 90 days to close, or up to 180 days, to give the seller some time to research other properties and be ready to move after the sale. This strategy helps you come across as an easy buyer, which is just another way to get ahead in the real estate world.

INSIDER TIP

Strike an upbeat conversation to learn key details about the value of a place. Ask questions such as "What would it take to do a deal now?" Sometimes they'll give the price they're looking for or provide guidance on how to bid.

Play Detective

When speaking with the broker who is representing the seller, you can ask questions that might lead to some remarkable discoveries. If you have the chance, you could inquire about the bidding activity. You might explain you're trying to get a sense of where the bidding is at. Not all brokers will readily share that type of information, but some will. Your task is to listen closely; you might learn that while the property is listed at $5 million, the seller has told the broker they'd be ready to settle at $4.5 million.

You could also gain insight on how long the property has been on the market, and the seller's mood about this time lapse. Sellers usually set a date for when they will begin to accept offers from buyers. An owner who has a property up for sale for a week might have a different mindset than one who has been trying to sell the place for two years. If the owner hasn't started to consider offers yet, you could reach out and ask if there is interest in a preemptive offer. This type of offer is given before the listed date that the owner has agreed on to consider bids. You could explain that you're ready to move and ask if there is a price that the owner would accept for the advantage of drawing up a contract now, without having to go through the bidding process with numerous offers from other potential buyers.

All these questions can help you avoid going into an offer cold. It might also save you time if the seller isn't motivated. If they say, "I'll only sell if I get my number; otherwise, I'm happy to hold onto it," it may be best to let that one go. If you reach out with very little knowledge about the seller, the property, and the market, you're increasing the chances that you'll pay more than necessary for the place. On the other hand, a bit of sleuthing and research will help you determine a fair price and see where value can be added.

Know the Landscape

Understanding some of the parameters of what can be done to a property before you step inside will steer you away from well-intentioned plans that simply won't work. Suppose you're interested in getting an office building that you want to convert into apartments. Start with the zoning codes, as they'll tell you what's possible—and impossible—to carry out on the property. Maybe you'll be able to redo the property, but you'll have to add in a sprinkler system. Or you could learn that it won't work to put bedrooms in the back of the building the way it is currently arranged, because it nearly touches another building and there isn't enough room for light to come through. You might discover that by cutting off the back third of the building, you'll be able to include the apartments you want.

Investigating the background of the place can lead to some great finds. You might discover grandfathered uses, which allow a building to continue operating in the same way it did in the past. The concept here lies in the fact that the property's construction, structure, and operations met the codes of its time. Then the zoning for the area changed, but since the place was already in existence, it wasn't subject to the new requirements. In this sense, it is allowed to carry on as before. Grandfathering can be a fruitful asset because you may be able to enjoy certain benefits that would not be available if you were breaking ground for the same type of structure today.

I always check on air rights associated with a property. These vary based on where you live, and they can provide an opportunity to build higher. Suppose you have an office building that is on a lot that measures 100 feet by 200 feet, so the building floor plate is 20,000 square feet. The offices consist of two floors, so the total space that is being used amounts to 40,000 square feet. You check the air rights to the place and find you can build up to 100,000 square feet. Essentially, you could carry out a project to build up an additional 60,000 square feet, which could bring in opportunities for more rents and greater revenue streams.

WALKING THROUGH IS WORTHWHILE

I met Margaret Streicker, the founder of Fortitude Capital and a candidate for Congress from Connecticut, years ago. She and I were fresh out of college at the time, and we crossed paths a week or two into our careers. I had just graduated and was new to real estate, and when Margaret was looking for something to buy, she came to me. She ended up becoming a client of mine and went on to purchase dozens of properties in the New York area through me.

Though our transactions related to the property she was buying, I noticed that Margaret had a unique talent. She could find value in places where others couldn't see it—sometimes even including me! She became an expert at touring buildings and envisioning how to reposition the place in a way that could bring a larger return than expected, either by implementing a new twist to an old piece of property or by finding buried information that only thorough researchers could unearth.

I remember one case particularly well. Margaret had her sights on an eight-family unit in Chelsea. When I showed her the place, I mentioned what I knew about it, which included that this property, like other multifamily units in the surrounding blocks, was generating a decent cash flow. (In real estate, cash flow refers to the income a property produces, minus the expenses attached to the place, such as debt payments and maintenance costs. We'll learn more about these in Step 5.) The place happened to be in a very prime location in Chelsea.

Margaret looked over the neighborhood, toured the multifamily building she was thinking of buying, and informed me, "I'm going to take this eight-family building and turn it into a high-end single-family home." She did exactly that, and those eight apartments became a beautiful one-family residence. She ended up with a great return.

Would a different investor have done well to purchase the eight-family property and rent all eight units for cash flow? Maybe.

However, Margaret found a way to add more value. She paid what other comparable buyers would have spent, but she came out further ahead because she used some inside knowledge—in this case, understanding the high-end area and anticipating that a well-off family would be interested in settling there. If the family could only find small apartments, they might not have chosen to move to the area. Margaret foresaw a demand in this type of housing, which wasn't readily available within the multifamily property sector. And she came out ahead in a big way.

Over the years, I watched Margaret carry out those kinds of creative projects time and again. At one point, she even took a large building and carved condos out of it; then she sold off the condos as individual units. Perhaps her greatest story—or at least, the one I like to tell the most—is how she toured a multiple-buildings listing in Greenwich Village, often called the Village, and made an enlightening discovery. The sale consisted of three buildings, which were positioned on two properties that covered a corner. Together the properties formed an obtuse triangle (obtuse triangles have one angle that measures more than 90 degrees).

I was working with the owner of the complex in the Village who wanted to sell. In comes Margaret, looking to buy. Now, as I've noted, when I work with a seller, I go out of my way to know everything that I can about the property. I want to show prospective buyers all the great opportunities the place holds as an investment and highlight its unique features. I thrive on finding ways to maximize the potential of a space.

Margaret joined me on a walkthrough, and then she went home and did her homework. She found a minute detail about the neighborhood buried in the 1,000-plus pages of New York City's zoning codes.[5] In her research, Margaret spotted an archaic rule that had to do with carriage houses. Who knows, the regulation may have dated to the days when horse-drawn carriages lined the city streets, long before cars came on the scene. (The Village was recognized in city records as early as the beginning of the 1700s.[6]) Regardless of how it started, the rule indicated that a carriage house could be built in the back area of the lots. Margaret took advantage of this right, and after she purchased the buildings, she added another structure in the back for horses.

I have to give Margaret credit for her ability to tour a place and imagine a new way to add value. When I interviewed her on my podcast, she shared how she built a town she called "Box City" out of cardboard with her brother and best friend during their childhood. Each kid used a refrigerator box to make their own home; together they constructed a town hall and cafeteria too.[7] Her projects brought out her creative side and led her to study architecture, a skill she brought to the real estate investment table as an adult. Her firm today manages more than 2,000 units throughout New York City and across the country, specializing in multifamily, condo, and student housing properties.[8]

Margaret's passion for design and quick eye truly brought her the competitive edge during every walkthrough. My advice to those starting out is to assess your own skills: if you have a knack for construction, envision new projects as you walk the staircases. By the time you finish, you'll have a plethora of ideas that are ready to be tested, and the winners could take your investment to the next level.

KEY TAKEAWAYS

- A walkthrough is essential to get an in-depth look at a property and pick up key insight about it; bring along your team to help you uncover all the details.

- Some environmental issues and needed renovations could go beyond your scope of interest. Watching for red flags will ensure you don't overstretch your finances and level of commitment on an investment.

- By striking up a friendly conversation with the owner, you can find out why they want to sell the property and what is most important to them. You can also get a sense of what type of terms they're looking for. Seek out win-win situations in a negotiation, such as a longer-term closing if the seller isn't in a rush and you need the time to get your ducks in a row.

- If you like to dig for information and hidden opportunities, look through the pages of the zoning codes and regulations related to a property. You may be be able to find ways to reposition the place or take advantage of grandfather clauses that your competition isn't aware of.

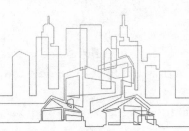

STEP 5

Initiate the Underwriting Process

When I interviewed Doug Marshall, bestselling author of *Mastering the Art of Commercial Real Estate Investing*, on my podcast, he agreed with me that real estate investing has significant advantages you won't find in other types of investment products. "Real estate owners have considerable influence over their investment," he said.[1] Chief among those advantages, Doug noted, lies in how you have some control regarding what you pay—and what you get back.

For instance, you can choose which property type you want to invest in, work with partners and others in your network to set up a business plan on how the place will be updated, reworked, and managed, and then keep tabs on it over time. Just like my grandfather did with his real estate investments, you'll monitor the financials and adjust as needed, all with the goal of getting the return you're hoping for on the property.

We've alluded to discussion on returns in the previous chapters. It's time to spell out what that means—and how to calculate what you might get from a property. This process gets into the income and expenses of the property and allows you to project a return you could get on your investment (assuming all goes well of course!). When you carry out this step, you'll formulate how much you want to bid—and why.

Let's break this topic into several components. I'll explain what underwriting is and its role in this stage. I'll also spell out how to define your return, which financial records to focus on, and how to draw up a forecast for your investment.

A quick warning before we dive in: some of the terms might seem a bit technical and tedious. Rather than viewing them as dry and boring—which, I can understand to a certain extent because it's a bit like looking at a dictionary and spreadsheet—consider them to be key tools within your inside knowledge repertoire. We've accumulated competitive advantages at every step thus far. Now I want to equip you with everything you need to know about analyzing the numbers so you can quickly read and understand important documents like a set-up, offering memorandum, and other paperwork that goes into the acquisition process. Having this insight will enable you to determine what price to pay for a real estate property, and it will help you get started on the pathway toward getting those returns you have in mind.

RISKS AND REWARDS

I'm not the first broker to recognize the importance of underwriting, which is used to determine how much you're willing to pay and the rate of return on your investment you expect. The process of under-writing goes back to the seventeenth century with Lloyd's of London, an insurance marketplace. Its founder, Edward Lloyd, brought his family to London in 1680. Edward was 32 years old at the time, and he saw coffee shops nearly everywhere; there were more than 3,000 cafés in the city, and they had a purpose that went beyond serving hot water that had run over ground beans. The sharing of news, along with business negotiations and agreements, reverberated within the walls of the coffee shops. Each place specialized in a certain business niche, and people loved to gather in them. It's where the deals went down.[2]

Shipping was a large, innovative industry back then, and sailors, ship owners, and merchants frequently walked into the coffee shops in London. With an entrepreneurial spirit, Edward jumped into this market opportunity, opened a coffee shop, and it soon became the go-to place for everyone who wanted the latest insider knowledge on shipping. The interior walls of his start-up featured extensive information about sea voyages, including details about the routes, schedules, crew members, and cargo loads for different ships.

Sailing was a risky business, given that so many things could go wrong during the voyage: shipwrecks, weather delays, disease, and so on. This didn't deter individuals who were willing to take on a bit of risk for a great return. Those gathering at Lloyd's would look at the ship schedules and issue coverage for the sea ventures. Every person who was willing to take a risk would literally "write their name" under the words on the wall that described the trip. They also jotted down the total amount they were comfortable giving in exchange for receiving a set premium.[3]

Off the ships sailed. If a vessel was damaged or lost at sea, the risk taker would pay for the repair or replacement, up to the total amount they had promised. In return for taking on this risk, the person received premiums or payments from the ship owner or individuals responsible for the voyage. Thus, if the voyage went well, the risk taker would reap in the rewards and not have to pay to fix a ship or get a new one.

Today, more than 300 years later, underwriting still has that concept—though we don't usually write our names on the wall or make bets on ships. The idea is to agree to accept a certain amount of risk during a transaction. When you sign documents, you're also expecting to get a later return.

Underwriting in the residential market differs from the investment property space. When you buy a home and undergo underwriting, the bank or lender that will be giving you a mortgage will verify your income and assets and look at your debt and property. They want to see how well you'll be able to pay back the mortgage, based on your financial records and constraints. When they issue you a loan, they are taking on risk, so they want to make sure you are a reputable and credible homebuyer who will be able to pay back the loan without struggling financially. They'll look at your debt-to-income ratio, which compares how much you owe each month to the amount that you earn. If your monthly debt is $2,000 and you make $8,000 a month, your debt-to-income ratio is 25% ($2,000 / $8,000). If the ratio is too high, the lender will often avoid issuing the loan because it exceeds the amount of risk they want to take on. If the ratio is low, you are more likely to be approved for the loan, as it is an indicator that you have enough funds every month to pay off your debts and have money for the loan payments too.

When investing in real estate, the underwriting process looks at the cash flow the property is expected to make. This will give the lender an idea of how much you'll be receiving from the investment. They will also look at the amount of return you'll be getting on the property. A survey of your credit history will take place too, to determine your credibility as a purchaser in the space. A bank or lender will use this information to evaluate if you will be reasonably able to pay back any debts you take out when acquiring the property.

INSIDER TIP

Pick a partner who has a strong track record with great banking and lender relationships. Over time you will build your own relationships, but you will first need to demonstrate that you have the experience to execute.

WHAT IS VALUABLE FOR ME?

When Doug, the author who has more than 35 years of experience in real estate investing, came on my show, he spoke of the benefits of investing in properties and maintaining them for decades. "You can see substantial increases in your net worth just by owning one or two rental properties that do well," he advised.[4] Using this philosophy, you could purchase a multifamily property and generate a return from the rental income it brings. You might later buy more properties and hang on to all or most of them during your lifetime. You then live off the income they provide.

During our conversation, I found Doug's insights to be fascinating, as I was taught early on during my career in real estate that the significant returns came on the sell. The strategy I learned was completely different than the hold-and-collect mindset Doug shared. You grab a piece of property for a low price, add value to it, and sell when it will get a high price in the market. If you're successful in picking the right locations at the right times, the theory goes, the big returns will follow. You could continue to buy and flip properties, increasingly looking to larger properties and bigger returns.

Which approach is correct? There isn't a one-size-fits-all in real estate investing. Both strategies have the potential to bring a return, but many other factors will play a role in delivering the final amount you receive. You might even purchase some properties to hold over the long term and buy others that you plan to sell sooner.

If you have investors, their expectations will also play a role in the hold period. Your ability to make a return, or promote, might also hinge on other activities. "Promote" refers to the portion of profit that a sponsor receives from a real estate investment. That promote could be dependent on a refinance to get better interest rates and loan terms, or it could be based on selling the property.

Just as sellers are motivated by various reasons to pass their property on to someone else, buyers come from different areas and will have unique takes on the same piece of property. You might look at a vacant apartment building that needs to be fixed up. You underwrite the property and believe you can get a 6% return on cost for the property. This is determined by taking the net operating income of the property (the gross revenue less the operating expenses) and dividing by the acquisition price plus the capital expenditures. You'll want to make sure the bid you place is low enough that you can achieve this return (and of course high enough that the seller agrees to the deal).

It's important to know the competitive landscape. As an investor, you may be competing against end users for the property, especially if the place is delivered vacant. Now suppose that a university is looking at the same property. They see an apartment building with no one living in it and spot an opportunity to turn the place into additional housing for their students. The university might be filling a need by using the apartments for dorms, so they are not concerned about receiving a financial return on the investment. The financial backing of the school will be different than the resources you bring to the table too.

In this scenario, the university might be willing to pay 20% or 30% more than you are for the building. When you carry out evaluations on the place, you see that if you bid that high, you won't make a 6% return. For the university, maybe paying more won't set them back financially, as their priority could be to solve a housing issue. The college might also have investments and resources in other areas, meaning their portfolio will be diversified differently than yours.

Continuing with the example, perhaps another potential buyer enters the ring. This entity is a developer, and they envision tearing down the building and putting in a new one. They expect a high rate of return from their investment. Therefore, they might be willing to pay even more than the university. In this case, the seller will likely turn to the third purchaser, as they are offering the highest price by far.

When it comes to bidding, be careful not to get caught up in the heat and emotion that can so often surround a sale. I like to tell buyers not to compete with developers as it could hurt their return on the investment. That said, perhaps you are able to buy a property, turn it around, and sell it to a developer who wants to demolish it and is willing to pay a premium to do so. You could make a quick, great profit, and then use the proceeds to purchase two more apartment buildings! You might hang on to these two properties for the remainder of your life, collecting income from them and building returns. It's always important to consider all the potential scenarios that could play out surrounding a property, as this will give you a competitive edge against others who may not be as aware or as informed as you are.

> ### INSIDER TIP
>
> Every property is unique, and investors can have different purposes for purchasing it, which will impact what they are willing to pay to acquire it. Know what the highest and best use for a property is, and whether your business plan solves for it.

DEMYSTIFYING PASSIVE INCOME

According to my friend Doug, "Appreciation is the name of the game."[5] On my show, he noted that property values have crept up in some places since the Great Recession of 2007 and 2008. In other areas, the prices have soared, reaching new heights and generating greater returns for those who purchased in the past and are retaining their investments. Drawing on this idea, he described how you could purchase a property and rent it. The leases could go up over time, which puts you in a good position as an investor to receive a growing return.

"Owning real estate is the best way to achieve financial freedom through cash flow, by generating passive income," Doug said. "The financial freedom occurs when your passive sources of monthly income consistently and significantly exceed your personal expenses. When that day happens, you no longer have to work for a living."[6]

The term "passive income" often comes up in real estate investment discussions. It is usually portrayed as a concept in which you can sit back and relax, and the money just flows in. You could be at the beach, sipping margaritas, while the checks are automatically deposited into your bank account.

In my years of experience as a broker, I've seen time and again that in nearly every case, the passive income doesn't come from soaking up the sun in Miami. When Doug and I spoke, he agreed. He stated that when he mentions "passive income," he isn't suggesting that we don't do anything. Rather, there is effort required on an ongoing basis to generate income from your investments.[7]

"If you're going to be an investor, you need to be hands-on to some extent on anything you do," Doug added. "I don't manage my properties; I have property management companies that do it for me. I manage my property management companies. I look at the financial statements every month and ask questions. From time to time, I go out and inspect property."[8]

INVESTOR TIP

Investing in real estate to get a return has some passive elements but requires a lot of up-front and ongoing effort to be successful. Even if you have a third-party manager, you still need to look out for your investment.

HOW TO INTERPRET FINANCIAL STATEMENTS

As you consider a property, you'll want to look at data about the place so you can get an idea of the net operating income that it will produce. You also need this information to see what type of loan the property will support to determine the remaining equity required. This will help you avoid getting in over your head; you don't want to take on too much debt and become overleveraged.

For on-market listings, a broker will typically send out what is known as a set-up. It includes the property information and financials (See Figure 5.1). This is often sent out initially as a teaser or flyer with basic information.

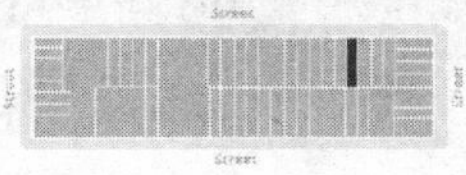

Figure 5.1   Sample set-up

Credit: *John Santoro, graphic designer at Avison Young in New York City*

However, it won't show detailed financial data. If you want to see more, the broker will ask you to sign a confidentiality agreement. Then you'll receive a full package on the property, which is typically called the offering memorandum (OM).

Before you sign your first confidentiality form, you may want to have your attorney do a review. This agreement ensures the seller that you will not share the confidential (as opposed to publicly available) information with anyone besides your partners, lenders, and consultants. An owner does not want information on their leases to get out into the wide open—especially to their tenants. Speaking to the tenants is also forbidden; this document protects the owner from the risk of that happening.

The broker will likely be registering you as their buyer in the process. Be sure to check the time frame on the agreements. You don't want them to go for indefinite amounts of time. In most cases, a year is standard.

In a typical set-up, you'll see a description of the property, the dimensions, square footage, lot area, a rent roll, expenses, and the net operating income. Keep in mind that oftentimes revenue will be projected if the place is vacant or below market. In these cases, it should be noted in the set-up.

Also pay close attention to the expenses. The broker should state whether they are estimated or actual. If the expenses are actual, they should also indicate when those expenses occurred. Beware of big line items like real estate taxes, which might be from the prior year. (Important note: if you are planning on doing a substantial rehab and greatly increasing rents and the bottom line, I would strongly suggest that you speak to a tax attorney to understand how much your property taxes could increase. In some cases, they could grow to a third of your gross rents.)

An OM should have more detailed information on the neighborhood, zoning, and transportation, along with photos of the property. It generally also provides detailed information about the tenants. The insight is often in the form of "tenant abstracts," which summarize the terms of the lease. The OM could also contain the floor plans, survey, and the certificate of occupancy.

The broker should provide a link to a data room. This is a virtual space (though the term "data room" can also refer to a physical storage room) where information related to due diligence can be stored. In it, the seller may have copies of the leases, floor plans, property condition, and environmental reports.

For an off-market deal, a broker or the owner might provide you with a set-up. However, it is more likely that they will give you a rent roll (otherwise known as an income statement—see Figure 5.2) and expenses. You can ask for a T-12 (trailing 12 months of income and expense report) as further due diligence, but sellers generally don't like to share these. This is because the past performance of the property might not be ideal. The same holds true for tax returns where a seller might include a lot more expense items to offset their income.

When reviewing a financial record such as a rent roll or income statement, you will need to ask whether there were concessions given to achieve those rents (we discuss concessions again in Step 9). Oftentimes, a landlord will give a month or two of free rent to entice a tenant to sign up. The tenant might expect that concession again when renewing their lease. If they aren't offered the concession at renewal time, they might look for a different place that provides the benefit they want. You can find these concessions in the lease signed, or you can look online to see where the apartments are being marketed. Concessions tend to be market driven, so following trends will help you gain awareness. If concessions are given, when underwriting you must take out the free month (or months) of rent to determine the effective gross annual revenue.

In addition to looking at financial statements, consult a managing agent to get a good picture of a building's net operating expenses. As we described in Step 2, this professional takes on the management aspects tied to a property. They might be involved in advertising and marketing the spaces available, establishing and extending the leases, collecting rent, and keeping in contact with the tenants. A managing agent will oversee the various day-to-day needs of the place, including maintenance schedules and required repairs. This professional may also create financial reports and analyze the property market in the area. For these reasons, a managing agent will have a firm grasp on the costs you can expect when investing in a property. Turn to them for insider knowledge on what the expenses will be so you can get an accurate financial picture.

Figure 5.2   Sample rent roll

										Page 1
										Menu ID RR
					Rent Roll					Printed 07/26/2022
					For the Period July 2022					

Building No:

Unit No	Rooms	Tenant	Rent	Chg Cd	Other Charges	Amt Billed	Move-in Date	Lease Terms	Date Vacated	Status Codes
A	2		1,506.55				08/01/20	11/01/21 10/31/23		R - RENT STABILIZED
B	3		3,100.00				05/05/22	05/01/22 05/31/23		D - DECONTROLLED
C	4		3,200.00				04/01/21	04/01/22 03/31/23		D - DECONTROLLED
D	2		1,836.99	110	VACANCY LOSS	-1,836.99			02/23/22	R - RENT STABILIZED
1A	3		1,671.53				08/01/20	11/01/21 10/31/22		R - RENT STABILIZED
1B	4		3,595.00				04/01/22	04/01/22 03/31/23		D - DECONTROLLED
1C	4		3,174.19				07/08/22	07/01/22 06/30/23		D - DECONTROLLED
2A	6		5,000.00				05/10/22	05/01/22 05/31/23		D - DECONTROLLED E - EMAIL BILL ONLY
2B	4		3,495.00				02/05/22	02/05/22 01/31/23		D - DECONTROLLED
2C	3		1,946.20				08/01/20	10/15/21 10/14/22		R - RENT STABILIZED
3A	3		1,405.23				08/01/20	01/01/19 12/31/20		R - RENT STABILIZED
3B	4		3,495.00				03/04/22	03/04/22 02/28/23		D - DECONTROLLED
3C	4		3,479.52				07/05/22	07/01/22 06/30/23		D - DECONTROLLED
4A	3		2,028.68				08/01/20	10/01/21 09/30/22		R - RENT STABILIZED
4B	4		3,000.00	143	CR TO RENT	-750.00	02/01/21	02/01/21 06/30/22	06/30/22	D - DECONTROLLED
4C	4						07/20/22	07/01/22 06/30/23		D - DECONTROLLED

Credit: John Santoro, graphic designer at Avison Young in New York City

DETERMINING YOUR RETURN

Once you've accessed and reviewed the financial statements, you can move on to calculating several figures that will help you see what you can ultimately expect from the property. These are capitalization rate, cash-on-cash return, return on investment, and internal rate of return. Let's look briefly at each one.

Capitalization Rate

Also called cap rate, this refers to the rate of return you'll receive on the investment before having to pay your loans and debts associated with the place. You find it by dividing the net operating income by the purchase price. Suppose you buy a property for $2 million with $100,000 of net operating income; it has a 5% capitalization rate ($100,000 / $2,000,000). If you borrow money, you want the interest rate of the loan to be lower than the cap rate, so that you are bringing in more than you are paying out for the investment.

There are two major levers when determining value for a real estate investment: the cap rate and the net operating income. The net operating income can be projected in some cases and can no doubt impact your valuation, but the cap rate can have an even bigger impact for determining what you will ultimately pay. For example, an investor who will accept a 4% return on an investment, as opposed to a 6% return, will pay 50% more for the property. There's an inverse relationship between the cap rate and the value. An investor who will accept less of a return will pay more for the property.

Determining the right cap rate is as much an art as it is a science, but here are some factors to consider along the way:

- **Comparable sales.** Knowing what similar properties in the area have sold for on a cap rate basis is essential to understanding where you should enter an investment and exit. Know the tenancy and condition of the asset to draw comparisons.

- **Location.** Cap rates in primary markets are lower than tertiary due to supply and demand. There are a lot more investors looking at New York City than Binghamton, New York. More competition and investor demand in primary markets will drive up pricing and reduce returns. Reports from Real Capital Analytics will provide ranges in various markets by asset class, which should help you.
- **Asset class.** Multifamily properties typically trade at the lowest (tightest) cap rate because they are less risky investments, whereas a single tenant retail property (unless it has strong credit) will command a higher return.
- **Tenancy.** The stronger the credit of the tenant, the lower the cap rate. A store with a lease to Walgreens will command a lower cap than a mom-and-pop shop.
- **The term.** An investor will typically look for a higher return for a lease with four years left as opposed to a brand new lease signed for 10 years for fear that the tenant might not renew.
- **Upside.** Investors will accept a lower return if the rent is below market. Conversely, investors will seek a higher cap rate if the lease is over market.

Cash-on-Cash Return

This figure will show you the return you're getting on your equity, which refers to the funds you contribute to the investment (see Step 6). You take the cash flow from the property and divide it by the amount of equity you have in the investment. It's important to know this amount because it shows you how well any money you've put into the deal is performing. Cash flow investors pay a lot of attention to this bottom line. They look at the cash flow divided by their total equity in the deal to determine their cash-on-cash return.

Return on Investment

To get a big picture sense of how your money will do, you can calculate the return on investment (ROI). Start by adding up the purchase price of the property (estimate if you are making a bid or wish to run through different scenarios), plus whatever it costs to update the place, plus any expenses related to getting the units leased. At this point, an investor might list capital expenditures. These are funds used to add on to or improve a property that go beyond the typical operating costs. For instance, they might include putting on a new roof, or the costs related to leasing the units. Then take the net operating income and divide by the sum.

Internal Rate of Return

How do you know if the cash you put into a deal will come back to you, along with additional money? One term that investors frequently use when setting up a deal and investing is the internal rate of return, often written as IRR. This refers to the estimated payback that you'll receive from a property during the life of the investment. It is shown as an annualized return.

Compared to the capitalization rate, which is a snapshot at the time of acquisition, the IRR shows the property's return over time, which is the income returned on an investment. It combines the profits and losses, the time value of money, and the potential future sales price. This future price is determined by using a projected terminal cap rate which estimates what the cap rate will be in the coming years.

Most institutional investors solve for an IRR when underwriting. (Institutional investors are companies or organizations with employees who invest on behalf of others, such as other companies or organizations). They might be looking for a "high teens" return over the life of the investment. This is especially relevant for value-add investments where the business plan is to substantially improve the cash flow of the property.

A property with an initial 4% capitalization rate isn't necessarily a better investment than a 6% return over time. If there is substantial upside in the 4% property, such as the ability to double the rents and resell the property at a 5% return, the IRR could be substantially higher from the 4% return property than the 6% return property, especially if the 6% return property doesn't have an upside like being able to increase its rents.

That all being said, IRRs are projections. My friend Doug Marshall is not a big fan of them, as they are rarely accurate in the long run and rely on future projections that can wildly change over time. The terminal cap rate, for instance, may fluctuate substantially and can be hard to predict. I tend to agree with Doug. I have a hard enough time determining where cap rates will be the next quarter, let alone 5 or 10 years from now!

INSIDER TIP

If you're not strong on finances, bring in a team member to calculate the needed figures when drawing up a business plan. If your proposal isn't sound, you could be looking at tight financial situations and even big losses after you close on the property.

COMPARABLE SALES APPROACH

The comparable sales approach involves checking your work to make sure that it can be substantiated. Think about this: an investment model can make the numbers say anything you want, but can your assumptions be supported? Knowing the comparable sales in your market is essential for your success. Your investment sales broker will typically provide some reports, but you should also study the various trade publications to understand sales in your market. This includes reviewing details like the tenancy, condition, cap rate, and the price per square foot for each sale.

If you are analyzing a vacant building that could have a gut rehab to convert it to residential apartments, you should feel good about your basis going in on a price per square foot. If your assumption is that you will fix the property up and resell it at 5% capitalization rate, you better be able to support that by finding similar renovated buildings that have sold for that level. When you develop your business plan for investors, you will need to include these sales to justify your investment analysis.

PUTTING IT ALL TOGETHER

Raise your hand if the word "underwriting" makes you immediately think of a large pile of paperwork. Indeed, underwriting is not a simple process; yet it is an important one. When you're starting out, you'll need to invest the time to learn the fundamentals.

There are great online courses that can help you learn to underwrite. Doug Marshall has a course entitled "The Great Game of Real Estate Investing," which can be found through my site (jamesnelson .com/resources). Some of my team members have found the course "Adventures in Commercial Real Estate" to be helpful (adventuresincre.com). Finally, you can take courses for a real estate master's program to gain a degree. Unfortunately, I can't teach you everything you need to know in underwriting in this book. You'll need to dedicate the time to understand the principles and methodology.

Consider it a quest to help you find that golden price to pay. If you do your research, you'll avoid overpaying for a property, which could cause a huge setback, as you won't generate the same ROI. Before you pay a great price or better, look around the marketplace and compare how other properties are selling. Bring this knowledge with you when negotiating so you have an idea of what's going on in the real estate marketplace and can position your bid accordingly.

KEY TAKEAWAYS

- Underwriting is used to determine how much you're willing to pay and the rate of return you anticipate on your investment.

- While real estate investing is often touted as a way to make "passive income," there is ongoing effort required to maintain your properties and reap your returns.

- A set-up and offering memorandum can be used to gain an idea of how much income a property will generate and what type of loan will be needed for the acquisition.

- Calculations of the capitalization rate, cash-on-cash return, return on investment, and internal rate of return can help you estimate the return you'll get on an investment.

- Check your going-in price by comparing your cap rate to other sales in the area.

STEP 6

Raise Capital

You've decided on a property type to invest in, built a strong insider network, found an incredible opportunity, walked through the place, and completed the underwriting. What's next? It's time to ask the pressing question: How will you pay for the place? This step consists of raising capital (it's also called equity), which refers to gathering the money to buy a property. Getting the funds together is something all investors must accomplish—or they have no project. It's worth taking a careful approach to make sure you have what you need—when you need it.

That's exactly what Jordan Vogel, the cofounder of New York–based Benchmark Real Estate Group, did in 2009. That year he made the first property purchase for his newly started firm. When I invited him on my podcast, we had a conversation about his experience in raising capital for it. He was working with a partner, and they had their eyes on two buildings in Greenwich Village that were being sold as a package. "One was 120 MacDougal Street and the other was 142 Sullivan Street," he recalled.[1] "The purchase price was $11.2 million and the project cost was around $13 million."

Jordan and his partner were asked to make a 5% refundable deposit on the property and were given a 30-day window to carry out due diligence. The two investors decided to split the deposit. They needed to put up about $600,000 (5% of $13 million) in all, so they each contributed $300,000. Thanks to the 30-day period, they were essentially given a free look at the place for about a month. If, after the time ended, they decided not to purchase the property, they would receive their deposit back.

They first spoke to lenders to determine how much they could borrow; they would have to raise the rest in equity. "We borrowed $7 million, and we needed $6 million in equity," Jordan shared. In other words, the two were looking for others to contribute $6 million in cash as investors into the project.

They made an agreement that involved what Jordan referred to as a "fill-or-kill" number. "Our view was if we could raise $3 million in 30 days we would continue with the deal," Jordan said. This was quite a goal! The partners reasoned that if they could find this amount, which equated half of the equity needed, they would use the time they had prior to closing the deal (which would consist of another window of time) to round up the remaining $3 million. However, if the two were unable to raise $3 million in 30 days, they would kill the deal and get the deposit back. The arrangement reduced their risk. If it was tough to gather the funds they needed, they would back out before they committed to something which would ultimately be impossible—or next to impossible—to fulfill.

To round up $3 million, Jordan and his partner brainstormed a list of individuals they could contact who might be interested in contributing to the project as additional investors. "The criteria we used was to go through our contacts and identify everyone we knew that we thought could write a $50,000 check," Jordan explained. "It was a true friends-and-family raise."

They reached out to 70 people who met the qualifications. Twenty-five said "yes." "Our largest investor gave $600,000, and our smallest contributions were $25,000," Jordan said. "Most gave between $50,000 and $100,000."

Thanks to their efforts, the two raised a little over $5 million in the first 30 days. They had crushed their benchmark figure of $3 million! It seemed almost too easy. Why were investors so eager to pitch in? Jordan and his partner thought it was because they offered their contacts something that was viewed as a dream opportunity: the chance to own a building in New York City.

"Most high-net-worth investors don't have a lot of options," he explained. "The average investor isn't seeing a dozen deals from a dozen different operators and taking the top one; they may have a desire to invest [in property] but most don't have any other real estate investments outside of their own home."

After this thrilling start, Jordan and his partner came to learn a quick lesson: no deal is seamless. "It doesn't matter how much you know going into your first building," Jordan said. "There will be pitfalls and mistakes."

For Jordan and his partner, as they worked to acquire a $13 million project for two buildings in New York City, the first bump came nearly as fast as the initial smooth sailing. Once they had raised $5 million of the $6 million needed, the two continued to reach out to more potential investors to see if they were interested in contributing to cover the last $1 million.

The two had a 90-day TOE (Time of Essence) clause in the contract for the buildings. This meant that they needed to close within 90 days. To close, the two had to have everything ready (documents, paperwork, and most importantly, the funding!). If Jordan and his partner were not able to come up with the full $6 million and close on day 90 or before, they would be considered to be in breach of contract. They would each lose the $300,000 deposit they had made, and not get the buildings.

The deadline neared, and the two were still short on funds. On day 89, just one day before they were to close, they were still $600,000 short.

The two partners scrambled to come up with the missing amount. It wasn't easy: they both already had put most of their net worth on the line for the deposit. They went back through their lists of contacts who had originally said "no" to their offer. They reached out to give them a second chance. As luck would have it, one of the people who had initially declined to invest in the project changed their mind and agreed to put up the needed $600,000. With a big sigh of relief, Jordan and his partner were able to close the deal the following day.

The lesson learned from the ordeal? "Raising money is always a struggle," Jordan said.

The good news is that Jordan, like the other savvy investors I've seen, wasn't afraid of confronting those hard tasks. He worked through each one and went on to carry out 23 deals with a group of investors from 2009 to 2013, raising $110 million, with the average investor contributing a check of around $100,000. That level of activity broke down into an average of one deal every nine weeks! His firm went on to do more deals, eventually purchasing over $1 billion in residential real estate. Through the process, he and his firm gained a reputation for unlocking and maximizing potential value in their properties, along with selecting highly strategic locations.[2]

One of the reasons I chose to include Jordan's story is because I think it speaks to important points surrounding this step. In my experience, raising capital is the number one process that holds investors back. It's easy to look at a deal, but when you need to drum up the funds to acquire the property, it's a whole different story. Unless you're independently wealthy and can pay with straight-up cash (in which case, congratulations!), it's a daunting process. The pressure mounts in fast-moving markets, where you might need to put $300,000 down on a contract like Jordan. In many cases, this amount is nonrefundable, meaning if you close, great, and if not, you're out the $300,000.

Clearly, there's a case to be made for playing this part of the real estate investment game by the rules. You need to know what you're willing to invest yourself and what you can bring to the table. You must keep tabs on the timing of the deal (remember Jordan's Day 89 crunch and dash to the end of the 90-day window!), reach out to others in an ethical way, and draw up the right partnership agreements. Let's go through these one at a time. I think in doing so, we'll ease those funding fears that so many feel whenever we bring up the topic of capital.

ALL-IN AS AN INVESTOR

I'm not implying that you put your entire household and savings at risk when you make an investment—quite the opposite. I'm referring to mindset here. I think it's important to be committed to the deal, in the sense that you want to take it seriously—and be taken seriously.

Brokers talk, and if you tend to make verbal agreements and then disappear from the scene, trust me, others will know. Suppose you tell a broker you're interested in a property, and that broker gets the seller to send you a contract. Maybe there were five other buyers bidding for the place and the agreement comes your way. It's up to you to get the money together and sign. If you can't round up the funds, and walk away from the deal, that broker, along with their friends and colleagues, will remember. They'll know that five other offers were pushed to the side to let yours in, and you didn't deliver. While the unexpected can arise—such as a discovery about the property during the due diligence process that breaks the deal—you don't want to be known as a person who can't pull the money together. If you show interest, are sent a contract, and back out because you don't have the capital, don't expect to get a lot more at-bats when it comes to brokers showing you properties.

In addition to putting in the effort, you'll want to think candidly about how much you can contribute. Perhaps you have $100,000 in a savings account; maybe you were recently gifted $25,000 and don't have to use it for an immediate expense; or you might have $250,000 in an investment account that you can easily access. Regardless of the amount, keep in mind that you don't want to invest funds that you depend on for your day-to-day living.

I like to say that you should always be ready to lose whatever you invest. Sure, we all want our money to double or triple—that's part of the excitement—but we need to be prudent about it. Market conditions change, and you don't want one poor investment to cause you to suffer financially or end up having to do something you thought you would never have to do, like file for bankruptcy, simply because you overextended yourself financially.

INSIDER TIP

Always be willing to lose the amount you put into an investment. You'll avoid overleveraging and have parameters in place to guide your next investments.

Sweat Equity

Don't worry, I'm not talking about workouts required when raising capital, though the concept of perspiring clues us into the importance of working hard to outperform the market. Let's say you don't have much cash—or any, for that matter—to contribute to a deal. There's still something you can give, and that lies in the insider knowledge we've been discussing. Suppose you're überfamiliar with a neighborhood near your home and have talked to every owner in the area. You're aware of up-and-coming properties, some which might not even be listed or known about in the marketplace.

If you find a fantastic deal and present it to others, you're bringing value to the table. Most partners and sponsors, when a great opportunity is handed to them, are just as much interested in the person who came up with the idea as the project itself. Now is your chance to participate as an investor based on sweat equity, which refers to a nonmonetary contribution that consists of time and labor.

Suppose you come across a property that a seller is anxious to get off their hands. You're told the owner is ready to take $10 million and you know the place is worth more. You've also made a connection with a potential partner who has a lot of experience in real estate investing and carries an A+ reputation for being credible and an expert at repositioning properties. You could take this information about the property to the possible partner and say, "I'll bring this to you if you, in return, give me 3% credit on the deal." You found the opportunity, and in exchange, you're asking for a percentage of the equity to hold your name. You agree that the partner will give you credit of 3% of the equity in the deal.

The partner is a master at finding capital and structuring the deal, so the two of you get to work. Your partner sets up a plan with $6 million in debt and $4 million in cash, for a total of $10 million to acquire the property. Within the $4 million of cash, your name will be attached to $300,000. Of the total equity, you get about 7.5 % ($300,000 / $4,000,000). The $300,000 is really your sweat equity. Notice also in this example that by negotiating, you can use your sweat equity to get in and gain experience. You'll be able to watch your partner put together the deal. You'll learn as you go, by observing the structuring and even gaining a return if all goes well during the process.

KNOW YOUR TIMELINE

When you're considering a property, you'll want to know the terms connected to the deposit. As we saw in Jordan's example of buying his first property for Benchmark Real Estate Group, the deposit can be refundable, meaning you're putting down an amount that will come back to you if you don't carry through with the acquisition. In cases with a nonrefundable deposit, your money is put toward the purchase; if it goes through, excellent, and if not, you're out the deposit.

The percentage, of course, also plays a role here. A 5% deposit required for a $1 million property will be $50,000; 10% would require $100,000, and so on. You need to make sure that the amount you need is available and ready to use. If you're taking it out of another type of investment, ask how many days it will take to transfer the funds and have them in an easy-to-access spot.

There is also the window of time before the closing takes place. As mentioned earlier, these could come with a TOE clause, which means it's essential to have your funding all lined up before that period expires. The window to close is typically 30, 60, or 90 days (and you can ask to see if it's possible to extend). Be sure to know how many months you have to gather the funding, and if you've never raised capital before, an experienced partner can come in and help ensure all the i's get dotted and all t's get crossed before the big closing day.

INSIDER TIP

A Time of Essence clause is a drop-dead date ("time is of the essence"); if you don't show up with money that day, it's over. Avoid these whenever possible and negotiate for extra time to close if needed.

REACHING OUT TO OTHERS

Let's start with what NOT to do. Please don't put up an online ad that states, "I've found the perfect real estate deal and am offering investors a 15% guaranteed return—contact me today!" Have you ever come across such a campaign? I've seen this done—and there's often a scam attached in the background. Whenever I read phrases like "guaranteed 15% returns," I think, "You're just waiting to get called by the SEC." (SEC stands for the US Securities and Exchange Commission. It's an independent agency of the US federal government and serves to protect investors and enforce the laws against manipulating the market.)

Rather than plastering messages all over Google, the process of reaching out to others tends to occur in a one-to-one fashion. Start by thinking about your own universe. Just as Jordan and his partner combed through their list of contacts as they structured their first deal, think about your network. You might start on LinkedIn, as it could refresh your memory regarding who you have met over the years. In your college network, there could be classmates that went to school with you and now have gone on to have highly accomplished careers. They might be interested in contributing from their savings or putting their next bonus toward real estate. These individuals, as Jordan observed, often don't have direct exposure to these opportunities and might be ready to jump in—they just need you to reach out and present the chance.

Whenever you bring a real estate investing opportunity to people you know, you'll want to explain why your deal is such a good one. Typically, a deal found off market with a good story attached to it (remember that estate sale story in Step 3) will get investors' attention. Maybe you know how to renovate it and make the place bring in higher rents, or you might have discovered a neighborhood that's getting vamped up and will be a sought-out place for families in just a few years—whatever it is, it's best if you can prepare two types of presentations: the conversation and the written document.

Know what to say to describe the opportunity in a way that others will understand. (Also: keep it brief! Your listeners will be interested in clear, direct information that gives an overview of the project.

They can always ask questions to learn more.) You might also put your reasoning in writing. Draw up a business plan so it's easy to see what your strategy is, the attached costs, and the expected returns.

You'll want to tell family members, friends, and anyone else you contact about the terms. In Jordan's first deal, he and his partner split the equity 90/10, meaning the investors had 90% of the equity, while Jordan and his partner had 10% of the equity. With $6 million total in cash, this divide resulted in $5.4 million from the investors and $600,000 from Jordan and his partner.

After putting in the equity, what would the investors get back?

"We paid 8% preferred return and took a 25% carry," Jordan explained. Through this arrangement, Jordan was agreeing to give the investors (and himself and his partner) all their capital back. After everyone had their cash, investors received an additional 8% annualized return, based on the amount they had contributed. Any additional cash above that mark was divided: Jordan and his partner received 25% of the profits, while the investors took 75%.

For the investors, this setup was fantastic. Some noted that the returns were greater than what they were receiving from their other types of investments. Indeed, they were thrilled to have the chance to outperform the market. For Jordan and his partner, it meant they needed to generate more than an 8% return in order to make money themselves. If they only managed to get a 7.9% return on the investment, the investors would be happy. However, Jordan and his partner would not have made $1 in the promote or incentive fee.

A quick note on the upside here. As long as Jordan and his partner could make more than an 8% return, they would receive a profit. This motivation spurred the two to dig in and find ways to add value to a property and make it run in a cost-efficient way. Their strategy paid off, and Benchmark Real Estate Group grew to specialize in value-adds. Today the firm targets undermanaged, undervalued, and off-market investments. These properties are then turned into high-quality residential housing units in their markets.[3]

When taking on investors, Jordon noted, "we did no special deals." For instance, if a would-be investor asked Jordan and his partner for a return above 8%, or better terms than what the other investors received, the reply would be "no." While it might seem that no customized offers would turn away investors, the argument could be made for the opposite as well. "I think others appreciated knowing that they were getting treated the same as everyone else," Jordan explained.

If you're working with a partner, make that apparent in the conversations you have with friends and family members. You might not have carried out any real estate investment deals, but by working with an expert, investors will see that you're working with a solid team. You could even show them the track record of your partner, giving them an inside look at their past successes. This gives them a chance to see how much your partner paid for previous investments, what they sold for, and what the returns were. All this can give peace of mind to others who will be working with you for the first time.

INSIDER TIP

Be clear with family and friends about what they can expect; treat everyone the same and lay out the terms in an easy-to-understand way. Start out right, and you could go on to do a series of deals with these same investors.

The final perk of carrying out your first deal with an experienced partner lies in the ability to tap an extensive network. If your partner has completed 20 deals, they may already have a strong stable of investors. This could save you from reaching out to hundreds of contacts; while you might still bring in your own family and friends, the task of raising capital won't be as daunting.

DRUM UP THE DOCUMENTS

Let's say you have some investors who are willing to chip in and provide the equity you need. Great! Now, how much debt are you taking out? What's all coming in and how will the funds be used? By the way, who will get paid back first—or last—when the cash flow from the property kickstarts?

This step can get complicated—fast. There are several documents that are worth drawing up. In addition to the business plan, they'll help keep all the figures and conditions organized and in one spot so they are easy to show others. Instead of trying to tally up the costs and returns in your own head, or writing them down on scraps of paper (or various digital files), keep the information in a few key documents.

The Deck

Not to be confused with the actual offering plan, which is the filing, this write-up is where you get to make the case for the property. A typical length for this document is 15 to 20 pages, and it will include various components. It might start with the broker's perspective. In my line of work, we create brokers' opinion of value, which contains all the pertinent property information. This perspective speaks to the value of the investment and includes comparable sales and rents to show what is happening in the area. This document is your chance to show how the project will go and lays out how the profits will be shared.

You'll put your business plan in the deck, along with supporting documentation. These pages will show investors why you believe your plan is doable. Suppose you want to purchase a multistory, 10-family building and convert the ground floor units into a restaurant space. You should have comparable rents included in the document to show what two-bedroom units are going for and what other projects have achieved. You'll also include the drivers for the project, such as a new employer in the area, population growth, or an influx of residents coming in from different cities.

Finally, this document will list your team members, who might give input into its content. Let those reading know you have solid relationships established, and that you will be working with an attorney, a brokerage team, a managing agent, or any other professionals that can contribute to the project and add value in their own way.

The Capital Stack

The capital stack outlines the equity and the debt. Think of it as a way to depict the layers involved. There are generally four sections in this stack and they have a specific order, starting with common equity. That's followed with preferred equity, mezzanine debt, and senior debt. Each of these layers comes with its own set of risks and rewards—let's see how they unfold:

Common equity: Though it is first in the stack, common equity has the lowest priority. This means that those who contribute common equity will be paid last. Who gives common equity? Well, you and I might. The sponsor, partners, and investors are usually the ones contributing to this section. They have "skin in the game," so to speak. They carry the most risk, since everyone else gets paid first. They also have the highest potential for reward; there is typically no cap on how much of a return they can receive, so if a high return comes from the investment, it is theirs to keep.

Preferred equity: This is similar to common equity but has some payment rights included. If you reach out to family and friends, you will usually offer them preferred equity. They'll contribute money for the project, and in exchange, receive their funds back, plus a return that will usually be fixed. In Jordan's example, we saw that the preferred equity was given an annualized 8% return on their investments, plus a 75% share in the profits after everyone had been paid. In terms of risk, preferred equity has less at stake than common equity, as the investors will be paid before those with common equity. Their reward, while generally considered to have a substantial potential, is also less than common equity.

Mezzanine debt: To understand this term, think of a home equity line of credit. If you own your home, you can use this line of credit to borrow against the available equity in the place. Suppose you have $200,000 in home equity; you can take out a portion of this amount and pay it back over time. There will usually be a credit limit established and a repayment period too. The interest rate is typically lower than other types of loans, so if you want to renovate your home office, you might draw on the equity in your home and pay it back over time, while you enjoy the newly furnished working environment in your residence.

For real estate investments, mezzanine debt is a hybrid of debt and equity. The lender retains the right to convert the debt into an equity interest if the debt is not repaid. As far as risk, on the capital stack this falls above senior debt. It has more risk because the senior debt will be paid first. The reward is also slightly greater, as the interest rate will typically be a bit higher than senior debt.

Senior debt: Listed at the bottom of the capital stack, this type of debt has the strongest priority when it comes to repayments. Banks and lending institutions issue senior debt, and they expect to be paid first. They're looking for a set return and a safe bet. Their risk will be the lowest, as payments are sent to them before anyone else.

Their conditions usually mean that they have the lowest potential for a reward. If an interest rate is set, that will dictate their return. This rate will typically be below the rates attached to mezzanine debt, preferred equity, and common equity. The senior debt is secured by a mortgage, or a pledge of the property. If payments aren't made, the lender can take over the property through foreclosure. They can then resell the property to recover the amount they would have otherwise lost.

Let's consider an example to see the capital stack at work. Suppose a sponsor purchases an apartment building. The transaction requires $10 million. (See Figure 6.1.) This breaks down to the following:

- **Common equity:** the sponsor contributes $200,000. The sponsor works with a partner who contributions $1.8 million.
- **Preferred equity:** the sponsor gathers investors who contribute $1 million.
- **Mezzanine debt:** the sponsor obtains a second mortgage for $2 million.
- **Senior debt:** the sponsor obtains a first mortgage for $5 million.

Figure 6.1 Capital stack for a $10 million transaction

Capital Type	Amount	% of Total
Common Equity	$2,000,000	20.0%
Preferred Equity	$1,000,000	10.0%
Mezzanine Debt	$2,000,000	20.0%
Senior Debt	$5,000,000	50.0%
Total	$10,000,000	100.0%

Credit: Derek Eakin, senior director of portfolio management at The RMR Group, Newton, Massachusetts, and John Santoro, graphic designer at Avison Young in New York City

Now consider Figure 6.2 to review the capital stack.

FIGURE 6.2   The capital stack

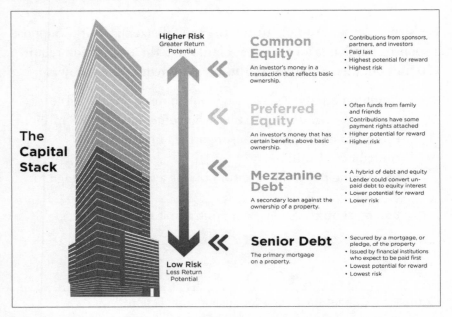

Credit: John Santoro, graphic designer at Avison Young in New York City

Notice how the image depicts both the risks and the rewards incorporated into the capital stack. As the risk increases, so does the potential for rewards (and vice versa). The capital stack is a must-have when raising capital. Senior debt will often consist of the bulk of the investment, but you'll need to build up the stack to see how the project is funded. It's a clear way to see how the returns will be distributed. It also helps everyone understand their position and level of risk.

Joint Venture Agreement

When working with a partner, you'll want to make an agreement between the two of you. In the example of the capital stack, we listed that the sponsor worked with a partner. In this case, let's say the sponsor came in as the general partner. The sponsor has insider knowledge, which can be used to carry out the operations in the investment and oversee the project. The sponsor brings in another partner for the bulk of the common equity. The partner will serve as a limited partner, meaning they will invest in the project but not oversee the day-to-day operations on it like the general partner will.

When I make investments, I often come in as the limited partner. If I know the general partner on a real estate investment is capable and has a great track record, I'll feel comfortable to contribute and then step back. However, we create a joint venture agreement first. This outlines how the cash flows will be distributed between the partners. Basically, you're making a contract that lists percentages to show what you'll each be taking from the investment.

Sources and Uses Document

This essential write-up serves as a roadmap to guide your raising capital efforts. A sources and uses document shows where the capital to acquire a property is coming from and how it will be put to work. The "sources" section of the document is similar to the capital stack, though the capital stack also incorporates the concepts of risk and reward that we discussed. The "uses" portion displays a breakdown of how the capital will be implemented.

Here's an example (see Figure 6.3) to get us started.

FIGURE 6.3   Sources and uses document

Sources	Total ($)	$/GSF	% of Total
Senior Debt	$5,460,538	$390	48.0%
Equity	$5,915,583	$423	52.0%
Total Sources	**$11,376,121**	**$813**	**100.0%**

Uses	Total ($)	$/GSF	% of Total
Acquisition Price	$8,500,000	$607	74.7%
Purchase Costs	$296,221	$21	2.6%
Total Hard Costs	$1,966,125	$140	17.3%
Total Soft Costs	$503,777	$36	4.4%
Total Financing Costs	$109,998	$8	1.0%
Total Uses	**$11,376,121**	**$813**	**100.0%**

Credit: Derek Eakin, senior director of portfolio management at The RMR Group in Newton, Massachusetts, and John Santoro, graphic designer at Avison Young in New York City

In this case, the capital is generated from two sources: senior debt and equity. This amount will be put toward the acquisition price of the property. The purchase costs might include due diligence costs, attorney fees, acquisition fees, the broker commission, and costs related to the title and environmental reports. Hard costs often refer to renovation expenses for the building and units; soft costs cover architect fees, marketing costs, leasing costs, and construction management fees. For financing costs, you could be charged origination fees, lender closing fees, lender legal fees, mortgage record tax, and other expenses related to interest, taxes, and insurance.

I suggest becoming familiar with the concept of sources and uses right from the start, as every transaction you go through in real estate will (or at least should) have a sources and uses document. Everyone involved, from the sponsors to the partners and lenders, will be interested in seeing the document. It may change several times as you go through the underwriting and capital raising steps.

Note that in the example the sources equal the uses. This is a key component to this document. While in real life, the sources and uses might not add up to the cent, it is a working structure that helps guide the process. I like to think of it as a fluid document. It will be used throughout the acquisition and beyond.

INSIDER TIP

Use a sources and uses document for your first investment, and make it an integral part of your business plan.

If you've ever purchased a home, you've virtually created a sources and uses document, even if you didn't call it that. When acquiring a residence, you have to think through the amount of cash you can contribute. If you need to take out a loan, you must consider what you'll pay the lender. You'll set up the terms of a mortgage and pay for other costs, like the appraisal report and legal fees. Adding these all up can help you see the sources (your cash and the mortgage) and how they will be used (transaction costs).

Here's how you can get started on the sources and uses document in the realm of real estate investing. Suppose you see a great apartment building for $4 million. You want to renovate it, and when you research the construction costs, you see that you'll need an additional $1 million to carry out the project. Your total is now $5 million. You go to a bank and find that you can get a 50% loan-to-project cost (the total acquisition plus construction cost) covered through a loan, so you have access to $2.5 million. That's your senior debt in the capital stack and on the sources and uses document. You now need to find $2.5 million of sources in the form of equity to have enough funds to acquire the place. You start calling family and friends and bring in a great partner.

You make the acquisition, but during the construction process there are change orders and cost overruns. Now the construction will cost $200,000 more to renovate than you first thought. You will have to go back to your sources and uses document and create a new total of $5.2 million (See Figure 6.4). Again, remember that the sources and uses must be equal, so here the money will have to come from you the sponsor, your investors, and/or the bank.

Figure 6.4   Total project cost calculation

Initial Equity	$2,500,000
Debt	$2,500,000
Total Project Cost (Purchase + Construction)	**$5,000,000**
Cost Overruns	$200,000
New Total Equity	$2,700,000
Debt	$2,500,000
New Total Project Cost	$5,200,000

Credit: John Santoro, graphic designer at Avison Young in New York City

Banks typically will not be quick to upsize their loan, so here you and your investors may have to step up to fill the gap. It will be very important that your operating agreement specifies what happens when there are cost overruns. You may have the right to make a capital call for this instance, where your investors have to contribute their pro-rata share of the additional cost. If not, their interest could be substantially diluted. This might change the capitalization structure and return waterfalls.

That being said, if you properly budget up front for potential cost overruns and have extra reserves in budget, you can save yourself having to come back to your investors after the fact. You should always factor in for contingencies. Typical underwriting standards for contingencies are often around 5% to 7%, and sometimes 10%.

WORK WELL WITH LENDERS

When you go in to talk to a bank about giving you a loan, you might hear a flurry of terms that don't make any sense to your ears. Here's the remedy: you can (a) work with a mortgage broker who is familiar with loans and fine print, or (b) take this book with you when you sit down with a lender so you can refresh your memory on the terms. Regardless of the approach, don't sign anything until you're 100% certain you understand everything on the pages.

If you've worked in finance or a loan department, these may not come as a surprise. For the rest of us, here is a cheat sheet to help you get ready for your first lender encounter:

30/360: This is one calculation that might be used to determine the interest rate for a loan. It assumes that every month has 30 days and there are 360 days in a year (not quite true! But it gives a good ballpark figure to go on, and it is a little less costly for you, the investor, than the Actual/360 calculation—see the following).

Actual/360: Another form of calculating the interest rate for a loan is based on the actual number of days in a month. It assumes there are 360 days in a year. Most banks use this calculation—note that it is a little pricier for you as an investor than the 30/360 assumption.

Amortization schedule: A table showing the repayment schedule of a loan, typically broken out between interest and principal, and showing the beginning and ending balance of the loan balance after payments are made.

Assumable loan: A loan that is transferable to a purchasing party in the conveyance of a property.

Basis point: A term that describes the differences and changes in interest rates. One basis point is 0.01%, so 100 basis points are 1%. Your mortgage broker might charge a point to close a loan, so if your loan is for $1,000,000 and you've agreed on a fee of "1 point," the broker will receive $10,000 (0.01 × 1,000,000).

Bridge loan: Can't get all the financing you need? This short-term loan could help you make it through the interim, until you get the final loan or funding secured. It usually comes with a floating interest rate (not another term, you say! Yes, this one's easy: a floating interest rate moves up and down with the market or an index, and the term is listed here in the "f" section).

Cap: This tool serves to limit the interest rate; it sets the maximum rate that a lender can charge you on a loan. If your loan has a floating rate, it may come with a cap, which will mean the rate can fluctuate but it won't go over a certain amount. If the cap is 8%, you'll know you won't have to pay more than 8% in interest on the loan.

Cash out: If you refinance (which would typically come later in the investing journey, after you've taken out a loan and started making payments on it—see Step 10), you might be able to take out the amount that exceeds what you owe on the loan. Breaking it down further, suppose you get a loan for $200,000 to purchase a property. Over the years, the property grows in value to $400,000 and you pay back part of the loan. You now owe $100,000. You decide to take out a new loan to cover the property's value. The new loan, or refinance, is for $250,000. Since you owe $100,000, you get to take the remaining cash out—in this case, that would be $150,000. Not bad, though you still have loan payments to make.

Commercial Mortgage-Backed Securities: Often referred to as CMBS, this is a loan option that might be available to help you finance your project. These loans often have more flexible terms and underwriting requirements than other types of loans issued by banks and financial institutions.

Debt service coverage ratio: Lenders may ask you about the DSCR, or debt service coverage ratio. This refers to the net operating income you'll receive from the property divided by the annual debt service. Recall that the debt service fees consist of the principal and interest payments.

Debt yield: Another common bank calculation, this is found by dividing the net operating income by the loan amount. Lenders will use this as they think about how long it would take for them to recover their loan if you default and they take over the property.

Fixed rate: An interest rate that will not change during the length of the loan. If a lender establishes a fixed rate of 6% in the loan, your interest rate will remain constant during the term of the loan.

Floating rate: As observed in the definition of the bridge loan, this rate can fluctuate. It typically changes at set intervals, such as every month, throughout the term of the loan.

Interest-only (IO): A debt service payment in which the entire amount of the payment consists of interest expense. No portion of payment goes to reduce the principal balance of the loan.

Loan agreement: A binding contract between the lender and you (or you and your partners) to formalize a loan process. Look for sections in this agreement that will indicate the interest rate and repayment period. It will also lay out what will happen if you pay back the amount early or if you default. If you put up collateral, such as your house, the value of the collateral will be listed in this document.

Loan term: The length that a loan will last. When you buy a home, you might have a 30-year mortgage for $200,000. After the 30 years, the $200,000 will be paid off. Not so in real estate investing. You will typically get a loan for less than 30 years and you'll make payments for the allotted time. When the term ends, you will still usually have money to owe, so you'll have to take out another loan.

Loan to cost: The amount of the loan divided by the total project cost. This can be valuable to lenders, who will view a higher loan to cost as a riskier investment, and a lower loan to cost as a less risky investment. For instance, a $250,000 loan for a $500,000 project will have a loan to cost ratio of 0.50, or 50%. If the loan is $250,000 and the project costs $1,000,000, the ratio decreases to 0.25, or 25%. If you have a low loan-to-cost ratio, you could get better terms on the loan than you would receive for a high loan-to-cost ratio.

Loan to purchase price: The loan divided by what you are paying for the property. If the loan is $300,000 and you are paying $500,000, the loan to purchase price ratio will be 0.6, or 60%.

Loan to value: This is, as it appears, the loan amount divided by the total value of the property. Lenders will usually have an approved appraiser determine the value of a property. If a loan is requested for $300,000 and the property is deemed to be worth $400,000, the loan to purchase price ratio is 0.75, or 75%.

London Interbank Offer Rate (LIBOR): Though you don't see this as much anymore, the term refers to an old benchmark interest rate that major global banks used to lend funds to each other. The Intercontinental Exchange administers the LIBOR, which is based on estimated borrowing rates. However, you'll now usually work with the Secured Overnight Financing Rate (SOFR), whose definition is later in this list.

Note: A promise to pay back a loan. (A short and sweet one! You're welcome!)

Permanent loan: A loan on property that often has a fixed interest rate and a term of a decade or more.

Prepayment penalties: Additional fees the borrower will be charged if the loan is repaid before its maturity date.

Secured Overnight Financing Rate (SOFR): A rate that is replacing the LIBOR as the benchmark interest rate. The figure is based on the overnight interest rate for loans and derivatives in US dollars. (Derivatives are contracts whose value is linked to the value of an asset; these contracts are bought and sold.)

SOFR is based on actual transactional history, and many prefer it over LIBOR, which is calculated on estimated borrowing rates.

Spread: This is the premium that a lender receives for making a loan. It is a certain amount above an index and is often expressed in basis points.

Swap: An exchange of interest rates, such as a switch from a floating interest rate to a fixed rate, or vice versa. If you start with a floating rate and want to protect yourself against rising interest rates, you might ask to replace the floating rate with a fixed rate.

Total project cost: As the term implies, this is the concept of the "entire bill." It can include the acquisition costs, closing costs, hard costs, and soft costs.

Did you make it through the list? If so, excellent! Keep these definitions in an easy-to-reach spot (also see the Glossary in the back of the book for more terms that are addressed throughout this book). They'll help you weave your way through loan documents, contracts, agreements, and professional service fees. Ask others along the way or refer to jamesnelson.com for extra help sorting out the terms.

As you venture into this space, you'll see that the capital stack can be as simple or as complicated as you can imagine. For the sake of comparison, suppose you want to purchase a property and you have all the cash for it. The place costs $3 million, and you're going to give the seller $3 million that you have ready to access from an account. The capital stack will be very short, consisting of your common equity alone. There will be no preferred equity, zero mezzanine debt, and senior debt won't exist. The structure will also create very low risk. No lender is standing by, with an extended hand, waiting for payments to be made each month.

Going to the other extreme, you could have layers of senior debt, mezzanine debt, preferred equity, common equity, joint venture agreements, and so on. All these can make the stack higher and bring in many different players. Everyone will be interested in what they're giving—and what they can expect to receive. Generally speaking, a capital stack with various levels of debt and equity will lean toward higher risk. There are lenders looking to be paid, preferred equity investors who want to see their return delivered, and pressure on the partners and sponsor to perform well—or risk losing a profit, or worse, a property, if things don't go well. (Thus, my ongoing drumbeat for the need to be prepared, have a team in place, do your research, be an insider . . . all these of course can reduce your risk when going through the transaction process of an investment.)

UNDERSTANDING INCENTIVES

You may find that buying in certain cities can bring funding support or other incentives from local governments or state agencies that are interested in restoring a neighborhood or improving a sector to attract more jobs. Some urban centers that—back in the day—served as trading posts or main port cities could be filled with structures that are no longer in good shape. They can be a prime opportunity for conversions. You might be able to carry out a renovation and turn an old, forgotten factory into an office building, or make an unused general store into a restaurant.

For those undertaking a rehabilitation, the governing agencies might offer tax credits or other incentives that can be used to help fund the project. Properties that are on the National Register of Historic Places are eligible for the historic tax credit at the state and federal levels. If your building isn't listed on the National Register of Historic Places but you think it should appear there, ask a professional to investigate. If the property meets the requirements, it could get added to the National Register of Historic Places—and you'll receive the tax credit.[4]

By the way, this Historic Places tax credit—at the federal level—has been put to work, time and again. It was originally established in 1976, and since then it has created $144.6 billion in private investment and preserved more than 43,000 historic structures throughout the nation.[5] If your property qualifies, you could receive a 20% federal tax credit, which you can factor into your funding calculations.

Check with government agencies and programs to see what incentives might be available for your project. Ask an architect or accountant about tax credits and have them show you the potential benefits you could receive. You might be eligible for other tax credits, such as the low-income housing tax credit, which is designed to encourage investments in affordable housing. The new market tax credit serves to promote the development of businesses in low-income areas.[6] Energy and carbon credits could be available for any eco-friendly developments you want to pursue, which can help relieve up-front costs and operating expenses.

INSIDER TIP

Ask about tax credits, federal financing options, and environmental programs to gather all your financial options.

KNOWING ABOUT FUNDS

As you build your capital stack, you may come across suggestions to start a fund. This is an investing option that takes several players to make it happen. Let's look at how that process might work.

I am a general partner in two funds: RiverOak NYC I and RiverOak NYC II. These began as a collaboration between my partners at Massey Knakal and RiverOak Investment Corp. RiverOak pursues opportunistic and value-add asset purchases and operational opportunities on behalf of a diversified set of investors ranging from institutions to individuals. It was founded by Steve Denardo, who ran a big fund at ING Realty Partners but noticed the opportunities for small to mid-sized investments that were below the radar. Derek Eakin, the CIO at the time (and who has also contributed to this book), helped identify and structure these transactions.

I had noticed this same opportunity in these small to mid-size investments, which we defined as under $50 million in total capitalization. We found there was a big mismatch between the number of investment opportunities at this level and institutional capital. Although 95% of deals are under $50 million in NYC, almost all institutional capital focused on larger investments. We would partner with best-in-class partners on value-add opportunities in New York City by providing equity checks of $2 million to $7 million. For example, in a deal where the total capitalization was $10 million, with $6 million of debt, we would come in with $3 million and our operating partner would come in with $1 million.

We had tremendous deal flow in an inefficient part of the market. If you are competing in this space, you will likely be up against a lot of inexperienced investors. Here you can truly have the insider's edge.

From my experience with RiverOak and relationship with Steve, I learned about what to look for in these types of investments for a fund. The following three characteristics are essential:

1. A quality sponsor
2. A great business plan
3. Location

RiverOak and Steve would pass on great deals if the team wasn't equipped to execute on the business plan. They also didn't like it when there wasn't a specific plan. For example, if the plan was to convert a commercial building to residential condos, the sponsor would need to be committed to that and only fall back on a rental plan if things didn't work out.

One of our most successful investments involved the conversion of an office building in Chinatown to office condos. The sponsor was Jonny Zamir from Keystone who had executed this plan before in the neighborhood, so we knew there was a proof of concept. It was also the right plan for the area as local businesses preferred ownership over leasing.

JUMPING IN

Sometimes the deals you remember most are the ones that got away. I clearly recall a time, early in my career, when I felt like I had to keep the great deals to myself. I hadn't yet learned the value of bringing in a partner and benefiting from their expertise—and financing leverage. There I was, working as a young broker, when I came across an incredible opportunity in the Chelsea neighborhood. An owner wanted to sell an eight-family property, and I was trying to get the listing. He flat out refused to bring in brokers. "I'm selling this on my own," he told me straight up. "I don't care what you have to say."

From our conversation, it was evident that I wouldn't be operating as a broker in the deal. This meant I wouldn't have a conflict of interest if I decided to act as a buyer. The owner was ready to sell the property for about $500,000. I knew from my experience and research that the place could be appraised for much more, and that his asking price was an incredible opportunity. I looked at my resources, as I wanted to pull together the funds needed to purchase the eight-family place.

At the time, I didn't have enough on my own to pay the half million for the property. Since I thought I should keep the opportunity a secret, I didn't reach out to others to see if they wanted to participate in the deal as a partner. I certainly knew people who would probably have been willing to go in 50/50. We could each put in 50%, or $250,000, and then split the profits from it later.

During the following days, I continued to ponder how I could come up with the funds myself. In the end, I waited too long. Another buyer caught wind of the property and swooped in with the money needed to purchase it. About a decade later, that same buyer came to me during my day job as a broker and asked me to sell it. I agreed, and this time, the new buyer paid $5 million for the place—10 times the original price!

By that point, I was wondering why I hadn't reached out to someone else when I first saw the property for sale. Surely bringing in a partner and getting half of the proceeds would have been better than the reality I lived. Through my waiting and silence (and hoping to receive 100% of the proceeds), I had gotten nothing at all.

The good news is that I had learned my lesson. The next time I saw a fantastic opportunity in that same area, I studied the asking price carefully. It was listed for around $1 million. I knew just what to do. I picked up the phone and called my friend Matt Blesso. I told him, "I found something great but I'm busy with my brokerage business. You know how to run these deals and bring in investors; let's do this together." Matt agreed, and the ending of that story culminated with tremendous success.

When I spoke with Jordan Vogel on my podcast and asked him to share advice for beginning investors, he said, simply, "Buy." He went on to explain, "Do it. Many people waste years talking themselves out of doing it, but you have to jump in somewhere. As long as you don't overleverage the deal, you'll own it forever." (By overleveraging, he was referring to borrowing too much and being unable to pay back the loan and interest, or cover the operating expenses because of the amount tied up in debt.) "I've never bought a deal where I didn't wake up the next day wondering if I overpaid," Jordan said. And yet, he moved forward and made those moves to purchase property.

One final thought on Jordan. After scrambling on Day 89 to round up a missing $600,000 he needed to close the deal, things got better. So much improved, in fact, that Jordan built up a significant database of investors. It got to the point where he graduated to a fund structure. In this arrangement, investors gave him money to go out and buy a portfolio of properties.

INSIDER TIP

Don't shy away from raising capital, especially from family and friends. Most high-net-worth individuals are looking for diversification into real estate with a trusted partner. Though it's tough at first, the process gets easier on your next deals.

Let me tell you, for many investors this achievement—having a fund—is the dream. You've moved from doing deals one at a time, complete with raising money every time you need it and panicking when it doesn't come through and the clock to closing is tick-tick-ticking away, to a fund with discretionary capital. Suddenly you can have the ability to act on opportunities when you see them. An asset manager will usually be involved in the fund, and this person will help you make investment decisions to maximize the return for investors.

In Jordan's case, with the fund in place, he and his partners could evaluate properties and move at the right speed, fast or slow. Investors were happy because they didn't have to do paperwork with every deal and make a deposit. And for Jordan, it showed his ability to build up credibility in the space and create a standout track record.

And it all started with that first capital raise.

KEY TAKEAWAYS

- Raising capital begins with an evaluation of your own finances, skills, and the timeline; once you know what you can contribute and bring to the table, you can move forward and reach out to other investors.

- The key documents that are typically involved when raising capital include the deck, joint venture agreements, and the sources and uses outline. Create a capital stack to outline the debt and equity in a deal.

- Many terms will come up when working with lenders. A few of the main ones to know as you start out include interest rate, amortization schedule, interest-only period, and term. Be aware of prepayment penalties, and check whether the loan is assumable for a future buyer who might purchase the property from you.

- Many areas offer a variety of incentives that can help you optimize your capital stack and improve the community at the same time.

- When creating a fund, the three main characteristics needed to make it go well are a solid sponsor, a great business plan, and an excellent location.

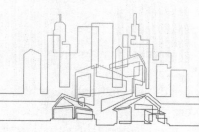

STEP 7

Close the Deal

ere's the scene: It's December 2009, just days before Christmas and the end of the year. On a cold night in New York, a storm breaks loose, and with it, the communication lines go down. Suddenly, no one can get in touch with anyone . . . and this outage, with the disruption it brings, threatens to prevent a deal from closing.

The deal happens to be a very important one—especially for some of the people involved, like MaryAnne Gilmartin, whose very career has been leading up to this crucial moment. Since 2007, when Bruce Ratner, the legendary figure at the helm of Forest City Enterprises, asked her to take over the project, MaryAnne had helped manage a group of 50 people who were overseeing the construction of buildings at Atlantic Yards in Brooklyn.

Or at least, they were trying to construct. After putting $500 million in the dirt, for a project that had no vertical building to show for it, MaryAnne and her colleagues at Forest City Enterprises faced intense heat. Their opponents argued that the plan, which included developing land for the Barclays Center and other buildings (and would go on to be known as Pacific Park) was doomed. The complications to this development project, which Bruce had originally proposed in 2003, ran deep.

As the clock ticked down the final hours of 2009, MaryAnne and Bruce knew they were nearing the edge of the cliff—and soon they were teetering on that very ledge. The situation was such that if "the construction for the arena had not yet started by the end of the year, we would not be able to finance that building," MaryAnne recalled when she came on my podcast to share her story.[1] MaryAnne and her team were working to close on a transaction that would allow them to continue with the construction project.

That's when a set of dominoes seemed to fall. The night before the closing deadline, New York went black from the storm, and MaryAnne and her team faced a dire set of circumstances. They needed to show government officials at the closing meeting the following morning that they had an $86 million line of credit from a bank in Cleveland. This would allow them to carry on with construction—otherwise the plan would fall through.

There was just one problem—and it was a big one. The document stating that they had this precious line of credit had been sent via UPS from Cleveland to New York . . . and it hadn't arrived. The whole postal system got backed up due to the storm. To complicate the situation even more, everything was shutting down—or getting ready to shutter—for the holiday, so securing other forms of financing was simply out of question. "We were in a moment of truth," MaryAnne said. "We were trying to close the deal, and we had to have that [paper] document in its original form or the government wouldn't take it."

Rather than giving up hope, MaryAnne battled on. She directed some of her team to try to convince government officials to accept a faxed copy that indicated the line of credit they needed was indeed on its way. She didn't stop there. "I was convinced if we could just get to the UPS facility in Queens, we would find the letter of credit," she explained.

And that's exactly what she did. How do you open a UPS facility in the middle of the night during a storm in late December? If you're

MaryAnne, you remember that one of the law firms that Forest City Enterprises worked with represented UPS. To her good fortune, the phone lines became accessible again, and MaryAnne called a contact from her network that she knew was involved in representing the postal company.

"He was in the Caribbean for the holidays," she said. "I asked for his cloak and dagger and if he could help get me to someone who could open the facility."

He agreed, and the doors to the UPS facility were opened. Amid thousands and thousands of packages, MaryAnne's team looked for the one they wanted. "At 3 a.m., we found the letter of credit," she said. This precious document, which indeed confirmed they had access to an $86 million line of credit, was handed to someone waiting in the car outside of the facility, who drove it back to the office. "We all stuck around and closed the deal the next morning."

Looking back on the event, MaryAnne recalled, "People thought I had lost my mind." She had also lined up a plane to fly to Cleveland the next morning, weather permitting, to get the document—though everyone knew the flight wouldn't make it there and back in time before the closing meeting took place. Through it all, "I never lost hope," MaryAnne said. "Sometimes you have to have to go where others won't."

Could that deal, which paved the way for the $4.9 billion megaproject of Pacific Park to be carried out, have been completed if MaryAnne lacked the tenacity to go to the edge of the cliff, and do all she could to get it closed?[2] Her sheer audacity and optimism paid off. She got the deal done, thanks to an eleventh-hour play of searching through the UPS facility for the vital document that held the fate of the project.

After that moment, Bruce, who at the time was running Forest City Enterprises, asked her to take over his seat. The request wasn't a light one. "If an article was written that mentioned him and the company, you would first see Bruce's name," recalled MaryAnne. Forest City Enterprises would be referenced much later, clear evidence that reflected the immense girth Bruce had in the New York real estate scene. MaryAnne did go on to become CEO of the company, and later branched out on her own to continue closing deals for ground-shaking projects in New York.

I'm not suggesting that every deal you take on will come down to the wire (though you should be ready!). Even in the best cases, however, there's often a sense of tension that permeates this step. After all, it's the moment when you get to take a property you've been studying and make it yours. Let's cover the usual pattern that needs to be followed to carry out a closing. This includes the offer, the due diligence process, negotiations, and the actual signing to finalize the transaction.

MAKING THE OFFER

Most sellers like to see offers in writing, as it shows that you are strongly considering the property. Preparing the offer on letterhead will help it to look professional. A good offer includes:

- The price you're willing to pay for the property
- The amount you're willing to deposit
- A proposed closing period, such as 30 days, 60 days, or 90 days
- The due diligence period (if you'll be carrying out due diligence on the property)
- Information about your attorney, which shows you are committed and ready to proceed into the contract phase
- A note that the offer is for discussion purposes only and is nonbinding
- An explanation that the offer is subject to a mutually agreeable purchase and sales agreement

Letters of Intent

As you become familiar with real estate investments, you'll find that some sophisticated investors prepare a letter of intent (LOI). This shows the seller that you are serious about making a commitment, and it typically provides you with exclusivity for a period. This means you'll be the only bidder allowed to consider the property during a set time. A letter of intent is usually not binding or enforceable. That said, there could be portions of it that are binding, so you'll want to draft it carefully to ensure you aren't legally committing to anything that could later come back to haunt you.

A good letter of intent typically has:

- A breakdown of the offer, including the purchase price, due diligence period, description of documents the seller will provide, financing terms, and the target date for closing
- A request for the seller to sign the document and potentially grant exclusivity for a set period, with a date indicating when the letter of intent will expire if it is not signed by the seller
- The names of the parties involved, including the seller, buyer, and those responsible for carrying out the agreement
- Information about the property, such as the address and size
- Financial details about the gross income, operating expenses, and net operating income related to the property
- A signal of a commitment from both parties to move forward on the deal
- Guiding points that can be used to draft the formal contract
- Disclaimers to note that the letter of intent is nonbinding (or to indicate which sections are binding)

When writing a letter of intent, start with an introduction that explains your interest in the property and the purpose of the document. Then outline the parties involved and their contact information, followed by the key points about the property and transaction. Add the disclaimers in the final paragraph of the letter and request that the seller sign and return a copy of the letter before it expires.

You won't be expected to deliver funds with the letter of intent. The document serves as a starting point for negotiations and is expected to be fulfilled in good faith. The terms listed could shift before the final contract is created.

Once you and the seller sign the letter of intent, you can move forward to negotiate a purchase and sale agreement (PSA). The PSA is a contract between the buyer and the seller at the point of sale that lays out the terms of the real estate transaction. It will typically list the sale price, information about the financing, the amount of the deposit, and anything that would lead to a termination of the contract.

Issuing a letter of intent can be advantageous. If you get exclusivity, you won't have to worry about other bidders coming forward and competing during the established time. Before you send out a letter of intent, be sure to have your attorney look it over. For the first few investments that you do, I strongly advise reading through every word of the terms. You'll become more familiar with the language and understand exactly what you're promising to do.

INSIDER TIP

Approach the bidding process in a serious, professional manner by offering your terms in writing that you know that you can deliver on.

CARRYING OUT DUE DILIGENCE

The toughest part of the closing step is carrying out the work to check on a property. You generally hear the phrase "due diligence," but this period is also referred to as the feasibility period or study period, or even investigative period.[3] A typical timeframe for carrying out this part is 30 to 60 days. You'll need to have the property inspected, and you'll also review the leases for any units that are rented. It will be time-consuming to go over the financials, but also an absolute must to get a good grasp of what the operating expenses will be, and what sort of return you can expect.

You may need to bring in third parties to carry out reports, including an inspection on the physical condition and environmental status of the property. If any issues arise, you could end up dropping the contract or negotiating on the price. You'll also use the time granted for the due diligence process to firm up agreements with your investors and lenders. You want everything lined up so that when it's time to close, you know what you're getting into and how to present the funding you've gathered.

For the due diligence process, don't be alarmed if the seller asks for a confidentiality agreement or requests to have early access to the findings. They'll want to know what's going on with the property, and it can work to your advantage. You might uncover an opportunity that can be used to lower the purchase price or find a problem the seller will resolve before the title comes over to you. There are no guarantees here, though. Unlike a home purchase, in which the buyer and seller will usually be required to come to an agreement about the property's repairs or faults, there's no law that states the buyer and seller in a real estate investment agreement must negotiate how issues will be addressed. On your end, you'll want to ask for the right to end the contract process if you find the property is not suitable for your needs.

Note that you'll have to pay for the tasks related to the due diligence process. There will be legal fees, and you'll have to cover the costs of the inspections and reports. While this is an investment of resources, the benefits can outweigh the costs. Check with your partner to arrange how the fees will be paid before getting started.

The due diligence process is a crucial component in real estate investing, as you won't have access to some of the protection laws that are in place for consumers when they buy residential homes. By and large, you and your partners will be on your own to decide if a property will fit your needs. If you uncover issues during this process, it might not turn you off completely from a deal. It will, however, help you gain an understanding of the work you'll need to carry out once the building is yours, along with how much money will be required to make repairs or take care of lingering problems.

Use this as a checklist as you carry out due diligence:

- Review the title of the property.
- Ask the seller to share pertinent information about the property.
- Inspect the environmental and ecological components of the property.
- Evaluate the physical aspects of the property, such as the structures and mechanical systems (if a wall is leaning, you should know before you sign!)[4]
- Do a neighborhood analysis.

Let's take a closer look at each of these steps.

Review the Title

You'll need to carry out a title search, which is a way of examining the public records to determine and confirm a property's legal ownership. This starts with looking at the address of the property and finding the tax assessor's office in which the property is located. The search can often be carried out online. Once the website for the tax assessor's office is found, the tax records for the property can be reviewed, along with the property deed. The current owner's name should appear on the most recent deed. In addition, the available deeds from the past 50 to 75 years can be sorted to establish the legitimacy of the title chain. In cases with records that are not online, visit the tax office and request the documents.

If there is a gap in ownership, an attorney should be notified. You'll also be interested in knowing if taxes haven't been paid, or if there are other outstanding debts against the property.[5] You could do this on your own or ask your attorney or a title company to take care of it.

Also bring in a title agent to secure title insurance, which will serve as an added layer of protection. The coverage will lower your risks and help you avoid a loss based on title issues. Another big reason to get title insurance: you won't be able to get a loan without one. The bank will also want to be insured against claims on a title. Consider title insurance an essential part of any transaction; it's better to pay a little more now and be sure that the property will be yours to keep later.

Ask the Seller for Information

To get an idea of the financial aspects related to an investment, request that the seller share the following with you:

- Tax bills
- Lease payment history
- Service contracts
- Financial statements and reports
- Surveys and inspection reports related to the property
- Zoning documents
- Governmental permits
- Approvals and certifications
- Architectural drawings
- Site plans
- Existing or past litigation pertaining to the property[6]

Remember that note I brought up earlier in the book about buying property "as is"? Keep that in mind when asking the seller for these documents. First, there's no guarantee that the owner will share this information (if they do, wonderful!). Even if they send over documents, you'll want to carry out your own research. Most PSAs include a disclaimer that the owner isn't required to show proof that the information shared with the buyer is, in fact, accurate and truthful.

I always recommend getting a thorough understanding of the lease history. You don't want to purchase a property with 100 apartments with only a set of assumptions to go on. For instance, maybe you can calculate the rent roll from 100 places that each pay $2,000 a month ($200,000 every 30 days!). Now imagine that 20 of those places are vacant . . . and have been empty for the past two years. That takes the estimated monthly income down to $160,000. Upon further inspection, it's revealed that another 20 renters haven't paid in six months. That brings us to $120,000. Add in the costs for managing the place, the bills that need to be paid, and the expenses that will accumulate to market and lease the empty places, and we're down to a figure that is much lower than $200,000. Perhaps the final number will be enough to pay your loan payments on the place and keep it running. Maybe the income won't be sufficient. Whatever the case, you'll want to think these details through before signing a PSA and making the place yours.

In addition, poring over financial statements such as the utility bills and operating expense statements can help you think about cost-cutting strategies. Now's the time to bring in a property management expert, together with your CPA or finance guru. Your eyes could be opened to new ways to run the property more efficiently. For instance, instead of raising rents, perhaps you could make the property more valuable by lowering the operating expenses. What if you can get a better deal on landscaping and maintenance by switching providers? Are there opportunities to install LED lighting and save on utility costs? Brainstorm with your partner and team members to find ways to save money, without of course going so low that tenants suffer or become dissatisfied with the level of service and leave.[7]

Inspect the Property's Environmental and Ecological Components

Where do you start with eco-checks on a property? Consider these:

The Phase 1 environmental report. Also referred to as the ESA (environmental site assessment), this report evaluates the current and past uses of the place. Your goal here is to determine if the property has ever been used in a way that resulted in soil and water contamination. If there is a safety hazard present, such as asbestos or lead-based paint, you'll want to know. Anything that is environmentally related and poses a risk to others will need to be dealt with either by the seller or by you and your partner.[8]

Transaction Screen Assessment. This is a lighter version of the ESA, meaning you'll pay less for the procedure. At the same time, it won't be as thorough and in-depth as the ESA. Consider the type of property you're purchasing and its surroundings, along with what you know about its past, to determine which evaluation is best for your investment dollars.

Geotechnical reports. These reports will show you information about the types of soil present in the property. The findings will also alert you to rocks that might be in the soil and could impact your plan for the property.

You can bring in environmental consultants to help you with this phase. When selecting a professional, ask questions such as:

- What sort of investigations have you carried out in the past?
- What type of insurance do you have for anything that might be missed?
- Are you certified by the Environmental Protection Agency (EPA)?[9]

Evaluate the Physical Aspects of the Property

You can have an inspector go through the place and check the roof, foundation, utilities, plumbing, and heating and cooling systems. You'll want to have an awareness of the condition of each unit and room and be alerted to any water damage or wood-destroying pests like termites. If repairs are needed, ask for quotes on how much it will cost to carry them out.

You'll also want to know what can—and cannot—be done to the property. If you haven't yet, examine the zoning codes to see how developments on the land will be treated. Bring in a general contractor and ask for estimates on renovations that you want to get started on as soon as possible.

Do a Neighborhood Analysis

Start by having the property appraised and then compare the place's value with similar real estate assets in the area. You may have started scouting the area (as I've recommended in previous chapters), and now's your chance to do a deep dive. You'll want these questions answered:

- What's the population and job growth been like during the last 10 years? Where is it headed?
- What's the median level of household income?
- What's the renter occupation percentage in the area?
- What are the property trends, and what have they been like during the last five years?
- How are the schools in the area ranked?
- What's the crime rate?[10]

Ask the town's land and zoning department to share a current plan with you. If there are other developments that will be going up in the area, you want to know about them. This is particularly important if they will increase or decrease the value of the properties in the area. For instance, if more industry is coming in, a residential area might see homeowners and renters move away. If a restaurant and shopping center is about to be developed in a location, it may draw a certain crowd to the neighborhood, and that could mean a demographic change in the coming years. Again, perhaps you carried out some initial research in these factors, but at this stage you want to know all the details before you lock in on the deal.

If these considerations start to feel overwhelming, there's good reason. Use your enthusiasm to find out the answers as a benchmark for value. For any real estate investment property, "there are about 100 variables," noted Paul Massey, one of the partners who gave me my first chance in real estate and now serves as CEO of B6 Real Estate Advisors, an investment sales and capital advisory firm with offices in New York City and New Jersey, when he joined a panel discussion on my podcast.[11] An investor needs to be on top of all these, but the thrill can come if you're in a space or project that aligns with your passion. When recruiting new agents to his company (and you'll recall that I was one of them), Paul shared, "We would allow them to pick an area they were personally interested in. When that happened, the results were better."

When looking at population growth, consider the type of market you're working in. In real estate, markets are frequently broken into three categories: primary, secondary, and tertiary. One way to define each is to review the Metropolitan Statistical Area (MSA) for a place. An MSA has at least one urbanized area with a population of 50,000 or more, according to the US Office of Management and Budget. It's the formal definition for a region that has a city and surrounding communities that are linked by social and economic factors. They are used to show which geographic areas have high population densities.[12] Here's a quick overview of what you'll find in each:

Primary market. To quickly calculate primary markets, you can look at the top 25 MSAs in the United States. New York ranks as #1;

followed by Los Angeles, Chicago, and San Francisco. These places tend to be heavily populated and have jobs available for residents, which make them both attractive to workers who are looking for employment and people who want to switch workplaces and remain in the same area.

They are known as established markets with large gross domestic products (GDPs). The GDP measures the value of goods and services produced in an area during a set period.[13] Primary markets are economic leaders and typically have significant opportunities for real estate investors. They tend to have high housing prices compared to other markets. On average, a primary market has about 3.1 million people (though I will note that the largest cities on the list have much higher populations).[14]

Secondary market. Often called "magnet markets," these are areas that are up-and-coming in several aspects, including job creation and population growth. A quick way to define secondary markets can be to mark the next 25 MSAs in the United States (spots #26–50 if you're looking at a list).

For real estate investors, this type of market can bring ample opportunity. Rent and home prices will be lower than those in primary markets, but these figures are on the rise, and people are moving in. The average size of a secondary real estate market in the United States is 3.3 million people, similar to the primary market size.[15] In recent years, places like Atlanta, Nashville, Austin, Dallas, and Phoenix have been highlighted as secondary markets that are attracting real estate investors.

Tertiary markets. Think smaller cities, with lower rent and home prices than secondary markets. If you're using an MSA list for ballpark figures, these would include all that fall below #50. They generally have a population of 1 million or lower and are usually not as well-known as secondary and primary markets.[16] As we've seen, the very fact that they aren't always on the radar of other investors could make them a great place to invest—especially if you know the area like the back of your hand.

Keep in mind that these are general definitions, and there is no set standard for what constitutes a better real estate market. The exact opportunities in each will be different, and the one you choose should align with the other factors we've discussed. Make sure you know the area (or are working with a local expert) and focus on places that really ring true. If you're passionate about helping your hometown see a revival, and the data that's available backs up your desire with a positive forecast for jobs and population in the future, you could have found an ideal location.

Finally, while these are general guidelines for the due diligence process, every case is unique. The exact reports and reviews you do will vary from deal to deal. Some parts are an absolute must (think title check!), while others may not be necessary. When deciding what to do, talk to your partner and the other members of your team. Bottom line: you should feel comfortable purchasing the property—and everything that comes with it.

NEGOTIATING THE CONTRACT

The PSA will be drafted and you'll have time to review it before signing. Comb through it meticulously. Now's the moment to put your findings from the previous steps into action. Any issues that have come up during the due diligence can be addressed.

If you've learned there is a tenant who hasn't paid rent in three months (or longer), you and the seller can work out an agreement regarding what will be done. You might insist that the seller remove the tenant before you close on the deal. Or you may agree that the tenant will stay and you'll deal with the matter. In return, you could negotiate a lower purchase price for the property, since you'll be losing on the rent from that tenant. If there are fines that need to be paid on a building, you might ask the seller to cover those costs. That said, unfortunately in my experience, the buyer usually ends up having to clean up the paperwork.

INSIDER TIP

You're responsible for carrying out the due diligence, and a thorough approach will save you headaches—and lost returns— later. Don't depend on others to make sure this step is carried out well; get into the details and bring in expertise when needed to gain the competitive edge.

SECURING THE FINANCING

The bank may be relentless when researching your background and inspecting the property. During the first time you go through this step, you can expect the lender to be very thorough. If you do repeat deals with the same lender (and maintain high credibility), this stage can become more efficient. The secret lies in the repeat business. Once lenders have experience with you and see your long line of on-time payments and strong credit, they'll more readily fund your next request.

When working with a lender, consider time to be an asset. The more you have of it, the better your chances of gathering all the material the institution requires and the greater your potential for a relationship. The longer you're with a lender, the more comfortable they might be to work with you, especially as they see you act with integrity and according to your word.

A lender will usually ask for some initial documents from you and your partners, including:

- Two to three years' worth of tax returns
- A personal financial statement
- A copy of your identification
- Your track record in real estate (if you have one)[17]

In addition, you and your partner can share an overview of your plans for the project. If, after an initial conversation, you feel the lender might not be a good fit, connect with a different one. Starting out right is key, especially because this type of relationship has the potential to be long-term.

THE CLOSING

Great news: once you get to this part, it's generally smooth sailing, as you're just pulling everything together. Ideally, any issues will have already been addressed, so there are no surprises. You'll work with team members—specifically, your investment sales broker, mortgage broker, and attorney—to get to the finish line.

When I started in the business, more than two decades ago, sometimes closings would take hours. There were adjustments that had to be made right at the table, and someone might say, "Let's pro rata the real estate tax payments, the water bill, and the sewer bill."

In real estate investments, to "pro rata" means to divide the expenses related to a property according to the proportion of ownership. For instance, the closing might take place on June 1, in which case the seller has owned the property for 152 days. The buyer will own it for 213 days of the year. If the owner paid real estate taxes for the entire year on January 1, and is now selling the property, the buyer will reimburse the seller for the 213 days' worth of real estate taxes that they will incur. The same is true for a water bill: if it was prepaid, the cost will be divided and distributed between the buyer and seller. Likewise with the sewer and other bills related to the property.

All these adjustments in earlier days would consume time as calculations were made on the day of closing and everyone gathered around an actual, physical table to close a deal. Then there would be more waiting for the wire with the funds from the bank to come through, and steps taken to ensure the mortgage was in place correctly and all the legal fees had been paid.

In today's world, much of this is done in advance, and the closing itself often doesn't take place in person. With electronic documents and signings available, the entire process has become much more efficient. Certainly, adjustments are still made, but most of these changes are done ahead of time.

INSIDER TIP

Don't forget to pause and enjoy the moment when you close; it's a big move to make and a sign that you're on your way to reaping the returns. Closing dinners are a great way to celebrate with the team who helped you close. Remember that it's the people in this business who will help you succeed, so show them your appreciation.

In my experience, I have found that brokers tend to celebrate more when the PSA is signed than when the closing takes place. This is because there is often a large amount of up-front work that needs to be done to get to this agreement. The document, as we covered earlier, lists the sale price and addresses the deposit. It also includes information about financing and the terms required for the sale to go through. Once the PSA is signed and the deposit comes through, it's typically a matter of waiting for everything to be finalized. (This is, of course, assuming there are no contingencies in place that might impact the closing of the deal.)

Closing is really the last step of the sale process and is a bit like tying up loose ends—by this point, the negotiations have ended, and everybody officially signs the paperwork related to loans, titles, and the like. The property shifts hands from the seller to the buyer.

Looking Ahead

If you are in good shape as the closing date nears—perhaps you have lined up the funding and are just waiting for everything to fall into place—you can use the time to think about next steps. If you're going to renovate the place, you can call up an architect to get started on the plans. Or you might connect with a contractor to begin filing permits for renovation or construction work.

One caveat here: before instigating services, check with the seller. You might not be able to proceed with some of the paperwork for permits if the seller isn't willing to help. If you have a friendly seller, however, that person might agree to file some of the documents so you can get the ball rolling on the renovations. Trust me, it's worth asking. If you wait to carry out some of this initial work until after the closing, you could end up with a place that sits idle for months until the permits come in. Meanwhile, if you've vacated the building so that the renovations can take place, you'll still have to pay some recurring expenses every month. Anything you can do to get started on the work that needs to be done on the property will help you move to the income-generating phase at a faster pace.

After all, adding value to the property is the step that comes after the closing. This is where you get a huge opportunity to be creative and put in strategies to outperform the market. I've seen it done time and again, and I can't wait to share some Insider Tips on what you can do to make it happen in your investments too. Let's carry on.

KEY TAKEAWAYS

- A good offer will include what you're willing to pay, the amount of the deposit, timelines for the closing and due diligence periods, and necessary legal terminology to protect yourself. A letter of intent will show you're serious about bidding and can grant you exclusivity to negotiate a purchase and sale agreement.

- The due diligence process encompasses reviewing the lease and tenants of a property. You'll want to make sure there are no arrears or issues with the tenants. A title search will show you if there are current violations on the property and to ensure there are no liens. You'll also ask the seller to share relevant information, check on environmental issues and physical aspects of the structure, and analyze the neighborhood.

- Once you've executed a contract, the work begins with the lender to provide the financing. At this point, you onboard all your capital to close.

- The closing is typically a straightforward step, thanks to today's digitalized and automated world. If the contract is well written, hopefully no major issues will come up when it's time to close.

STEP 8

Reposition the Property

L et this horror story be an example of how we can learn from our mistakes: During my initial days of purchasing properties as an investment, I found an apartment building in Connecticut that caught my eye. In previous chapters, I've emphasized the importance of knowing an area where you invest, and the property checked that box, as I was living in Connecticut at the time. I ran the numbers. They looked perfect! I thought I could readily bring in a 7% or 8% return. "Easy," I said to myself. "I'm going to buy this and make money in my sleep."

I went in on my own for the deal . . . and the nightmares soon followed. It was a total disaster. The tenants brought me one challenge after another. Among them was the fact that a lot of the residents simply stopped paying rent. Obviously, this impacted the rent roll, and my income from the place plunged. It had looked ideal on paper, but it was far from pleasant to deal with and financially it was a big loss. I had to bring in an attorney to get some of the tenants to move out. The promise of a great return had turned out to be a mere façade.

What had I done wrong? As I reflected on the turn of events, I realized I had gone outside of my area of expertise. I didn't have much experience managing an apartment building, and I wasn't ready for the time commitment it required. I also didn't have a strong grasp of how to manage it. Those books and articles I had read that assured me the passive income would magically appear after I closed the deal didn't seem accurate in my case.

I don't want those misfortunes to fall your way either. I picked myself up, fixed the apartment building and tenant situation, and got out of the mess. I went on to make better decisions in the next deals, as I had a clearer understanding of what to do and what to avoid. I knew that while numbers can look enticing on paper, it takes hard work and effort to turn them into a reality.

The experience helped me gain a better grasp of the importance of managing a property to get a return. Moreover, throughout my career I've seen that there are different ways to create value and walk away with gains. By the time you reach this step, chances are you'll have thought about what you want to do with your investment property (and if you haven't, now is the time to start!).

Part of your business plan will likely include the changes you want to make to the structure or how you want to improve efficiencies. Ultimately, you're looking for a return that you and the others involved are satisfied to see. There are basic expenses to take care of, and we've observed how loans will need to be repaid to lenders, who typically get the first cut of any profits. That's why it's important to generate value that surpasses these initial paybacks and moves the needle to other areas. You want the cash to flow to your investors and partners too.

One more personal side note before we move on: I want to point out that part of the return in an investment can go beyond the financial success. Many times, there are gratifying moments along the way, and I get a sense of purpose every time I walk through a neighborhood that I have helped to improve. If I see one of my buildings being used by a tenant who is thriving, as a result of my efforts in the transactions and deal, it's meaningful to me.

With that in mind, let's look at the different ways to add value, including bringing in a property manager and running the property efficiently. We'll delve into repositioning the place, which can increase its sale price in the future. Finally, we'll cover ways that pursuing a passion can bring a sentimental return that goes above the financial records.

THE BENEFITS OF A PROPERTY MANAGER

I'll be the first one to advocate for bringing in help to operate a real estate investment. Think about it from a practical point of view: Are you interested in making this your full-time job? Even if the answer is "yes," you might not want to leave your present position and risk losing out on your current income, especially if your budget depends on that monthly salary.

Interestingly, I've met real estate investors who started out as full-time property managers for a firm before they made a real estate investment on their own. (Property managers are sometimes called third-party managers or managing agents, which we noted in Step 2.) These individuals had the benefit of bringing in a paycheck while they learned the ropes of the trade. Once they felt comfortable with the knowledge they had gained, they branched out on their own.

In my line of work, I often see investors self-manage properties when they start. They think, "I can't afford to pay a third-party manager." Cost-wise, a property manager might charge anywhere from 3% to 6% on the gross revenue of a place (though this can vary depending on the market you're in). Suppose you own a building that has an annual rent roll of $200,000. If you're paying a property manager 5%, you'll be handing out $10,000 a year (0.05 × $200,000).

Following this example, I tend to ask, "Is your time worth more than $10,000 a year?" If you're managing the place, you'll spend hours and hours overseeing the details of it. You also won't have the insider knowledge that an experienced property manager can bring to the table. Think of someone who has run properties for the past 20 years. They'll be familiar with ways to keep expenses down, and they'll have strong relationships with gas suppliers, oil companies, insurance providers, handymen, painters, electricians, plumbers, and so on. They have avenues available to save you money on operating costs that wouldn't be accessible if you were in their shoes. Experienced managing agents will also have bargaining power they can use. Suppose a managing agent runs 1,000 units over 50 buildings; that agent can likely negotiate some favorable terms with providers, as they'll be able to leverage the amount of business they can generate to service people for lower rates.

INSIDER TIP

Evaluate the value of your time when managing property—don't run cheap and try to do it on your own if you don't have the bandwidth and expertise.

Still, it's true that if you self-manage, no one will work harder for the building than you. That property manager that's overseeing 50 buildings probably isn't completely focused on what's the absolute best for yours. If you're in on the day-to-day operations, you can tackle issues that come up right away, get to know the tenants and build relationships with them, and stay tuned in to ways to improve the property.

When looking for a property manager, search for one that provides the services you need. Their duties can vary, and often include:

- Collecting rent
- Handling maintenance requests
- Filling vacant units

- Creating monthly reports that show rent income and expenses
- Overseeing construction projects

If you take on a property manager, ask them for their opinion about the operations of the place. Here's your chance to learn how efficiencies can be created and get ideas to increase the value. If they have an eye for detail or are skilled with numbers, they could offer you insight that could impact the overall financial performance of the place.

Neighborhood Expertise

My friend Jeff Ravetz began his career at Time Equities, which has grown to be a global real estate investment and development firm. When he joined, however, the company focused on New York. In his position in the finance department, Jeff had the chance to view the dollar signs attached to different projects. As he observed firms in the industry that were dipping into other regions of the country, he noticed that being a new kid on the block and acting alone did not bring significant returns in the area of property management.

When Time Equities looked at expanding into Texas, Jeff knew the company's chance of success would be low (or nonexistent) if they tried to do everything on their own. "We were sensitive to the fact that we didn't know the area and needed local expertise," Jeff explained on my podcast.[1] So, they hired a managing agent who knew the Texas market, understood the rent prices, and had an intuitive sense of the nuances of the area. The method worked so well that Jeff's firm replicated this model of hiring a local managing agent as they expanded into other areas of the country.

"Later on in my career, when I started Lighthouse Real Estate Ventures with friends, we invested in Long Island, which is where I'm from," he shared. For those deals, he had more input to bring to the table. "It's so important to understand the geographical area. If you don't know the strengths of the market where you're investing, you can get hurt by thinking the structure makes sense," he added.[2] "You might not be able to rent the space for the appropriate income."

Know the Limits

While a property manager can bring efficiencies and save you time, keep in mind that you are ultimately more invested in the building and its tenants. No one will care as much about your investments as you do! A top-notch property manager can be like a solid right hand. They will contribute greatly to the return, but they won't have the final say in what is done with the property.

THE POTENTIAL OF A VALUE-ADD PROPERTY

In Step 1, we looked at four main types of real estate investments based on the risk you want to assume. As a quick refresher, these are core investment, core plus, value-add, and opportunistic. I mentioned that a core investment is typically a property in a high-quality location, such as a well-trafficked, heavily populated area. The tenants tend to be high-quality too, which means they have a low risk of leaving and a strong credit background. Think of national retailers like CVS, Starbucks, Walgreens, or McDonald's. These properties typically have predictable cash flows and the tenants generally oversee all the upkeep and repairs. You usually won't have to deal with renovations or bringing on new tenants. If you invest in this type of property, you might get a 10-year lease and receive a rent check the first of every month. The returns may not be as favorable in fluctuating markets, such as periods of inflation. Suppose you're two years in to a 10-year lease and the rent is set for the next eight years. If prices rise in the area, the return may not be as high as you envisioned when you took on the property.

We also looked at core plus, which involves a property that is usually already cash flowing and might only need some light repairs and touch-ups. The returns here could be better than a core investment, but the chance for a greater upside isn't as high as the other two categories of value-add and opportunistic. I pointed out the challenges of opportunistic, which could have phenomenal returns but requires major lifting and financing up front, and thus makes it a less than ideal choice for first-time investors.

This brings us to value-add properties, which are intricate and worth breaking down a bit more here. When we speak of this type of investment, I always think of significant changes like big renovation projects, new uses for the space, sweeping improvements on record keeping, and the like. This is your chance to take a property and move it to a new level . . . one that brings those game-changing returns we've been highlighting.

If you find a place that you can position differently in some way to get a greater return, you'll be on your way to outperforming the market. This concept often plays out in the real world when an investor takes a property that has been mismanaged for a long time and isn't producing its full potential. Maybe an owner didn't maximize rents or hasn't changed the place in 20 years, and it could use some renovations that would bring in higher-paying tenants.

You would be surprised how often I see value-add opportunities. It's not uncommon for me to come across two apartment buildings that are right next door to each other. They were both built at the same time and are currently offering one-bedroom units. Take a closer look and you'll find that one place is asking $3,800 a month for an apartment and the other building has rents set at $5,000. "Why the discrepancy?" You ask. Then you walk into the $5,000 per month place, and you're met with a beautiful, well-lit lobby. The apartments are plush with washers and dryers, granite countertops, and stainless-steel appliances, among other amenities. You've just found your answer to the question on price differences.

Applying this example to the value-add space we can see that making a place nicer can increase the rent roll. The changes must always be weighed financially and in accordance with the market.

Perhaps you have a one-bedroom 30-year-old apartment unit that you want to gut and make to look like new. Your rental broker tells you that to maximize rent, you should convert the unit from a one bedroom to a two bedroom and include stainless steel appliances, a stone countertop, a new tile bathroom, new hardwood floors, and a washer and dryer. Your architect draws up plans so your general contractor can give you a bid.

The work will cost you $50,000 to renovate. If you carry out the project, your rental broker tells you that you'll be able to increase the rent from $2,000 to $3,500 a month. Let's see if this is a good return on your investment.

It will take you three months to renovate with a loss of rent, but it will bring you an additional $18,000 of rent a year. If you value that income at a 6% capitalization rate, that's $300,000 in additional value. On a $50,000 investment, that's a 16.6% return on investment. (See Figure 8.1.) Not a bad exercise! (Quick caveat: financial gurus will point out the additional costs like taxes that have to be included. For the sake of simplicity, we'll leave the example as it is, and note that even when you take out the additional expenses, you'll come out ahead more than if you hadn't renovated.)

Another lens that can be used to view this value-add project is the sales price. Suppose you renovate for $50,000 and then have the place appraised. You learn that the apartment is now worth $120,000 more. Your input of $50,000 could bring a sale that is 2.4 times the amount. Again, there will be other expenses to consider; however, I think we can safely say that the value has definitely been increased!

Figure 8.1 Return on investment calculation

Current Monthly Rent	$2,000
Projected Monthly Rent	$3,500
Annual Potential Increase	$18,000
Increased Capitalized Value: ($18,000 / 6%)	$300,000
Renovation Cost	$50,000
Return On Investment: ($50,000/$300,000)	16.60%

Credit: John Santoro, graphic designer at Avison Young in New York City

I personally love to find opportunities in mixed use spaces, such as a property with retail space on the ground floor and apartments above. Multifamily assets, as we've seen, tend to be lower risk; after all, people always need a place to live. Retail is typically riskier, so the two can balance each other out. Find a mixed-use property with some apartments that are underpriced and a retail space that could be changed up to suit new businesses that are flocking to the area, and you'll have my ear.

In value-add properties, you might not be the one drawing up new design plans, swinging the hammer on a construction site, or analyzing hundreds of pages of financial statements to find ways to reduce expenses. You'll be involved in some way, and that might be as a sponsor, where you orchestrate the work of others who are utilizing their area of expertise to add value. Or you could be working with a partner who has experience in adding value. If that person takes the reigns, you can go along for the ride to learn how it's done and then apply those techniques to your next investment.

CONSTRUCTION THE RIGHT WAY

Hopefully by now you've had an architect come in and look the place over—if you're going to do some renovations. Whether you're turning two-bedroom condos into three-bedroom units or creating some additional retail space, the idea is to hit the ground running after you close. As a quick review, before you start a construction project, be sure to first:

- Speak to rental brokers and residential brokers to learn what the demand is in the area.
- Have a solid idea of your target tenant. (Are you catering to young professionals who will share a two-bedroom apartment? A family who will want a larger living area and bedrooms?)
- Position yourself in the market. (Are you going to turn a sleepy old hardware store into a restaurant? Will you add some garden space to a café for outdoor seating to coincide with an open-air eating trend?)
- Meet with architects and general contractors to draw up project plans.

This vetting process will help you sort through ideas and find the one that can add value in a practical way. I remember at one point, I thought I knew a perfect addition to the town where I live. I had this amazing dream of building a taqueria and tequila bar. I found a space on a main street and said to others, "Wouldn't it be great if we could open up a restaurant here?" I couldn't wait to dig in.

Fortunately, I've also been in this business long enough to know that I should ask questions first. When I looked into the town's parking requirements, I realized there was no parking available for the restaurant. Moreover, the city prohibited restaurants from opening if they didn't have designated parking for customers. Needless to say, there's no taqueria and tequila bar in my town, and had I tried, I would have lost a great deal of capital because the investment would have gone nowhere. And now, I'm sharing this story with you so you can avoid the same mistakes!

Bear in mind that cost overruns related to construction can crush your investment, even if it's been a solid ride up to this point. That's because throughout the bidding and acquisition process, your expenses remain controlled to a certain extent. Once you get into ordering supplies and working with a contractor, the fees can escalate faster than you might think. There are different contracts you can take out, and you'll want to consider which one will mitigate your risks. Here are a couple common ones you'll see:

Guaranteed maximum price (GMP) contract. This type of agreement includes an all-in number, which caps the amount you'll spend on the project. It will often list a delivery date, with an understanding that the project will be completed by the listed day. If it is not finished when the deadline hits, the contractor will pay a penalty. Alternatively, for a project delivered early, you might include a bonus.

Open shop contract. This plan doesn't have a capped number that indicates a ceiling to how much the project will cost. It indicates that bids will be placed for each aspect of the project. This allows professionals to offer their best prices for services like plumbing, electricity, and so on. The advantage here is that the open plan provides you with a chance to get reduced prices for the work. Without a cap in place, though, you could end up paying more than you bargained for in the long run.

I love the old saying "The squeaky wheel gets the oil," and it certainly applies to construction projects. If you're only showing up to the job site once a month, you're not going to know as much about what's going on compared to visiting once or twice a week. I advocate having a weekly meeting at the construction site to walk through the property and see how everyone's moving.

During these visits, you can discuss the tasks at hand with the general contractor and look at next steps. Toward the end of a project, a punch list is often created. This is a document that outlines the minor repairs, fixes, or jobs that must be carried out or resolved for the work to be considered complete. Your on-site presence will help minor bumps and delays get sorted out quickly, which can keep the project on track.

THE GREAT SENSE OF GRATIFICATION

When I interviewed my friend Jeff Ravetz, who by then was principal of Girona Ventures, on my podcast, I asked him to share some of his most successful stories. After naming a couple of outstanding financial accomplishments, he moved on to share what one of his most gratifying experiences has been. "My partner and I have been part of the transformation of a city," he said, with a hint of pride.[3]

> **INSIDER TIP**
>
> Some of the greatest returns might stem from contributing to projects that improve the wellbeing of citizens and communities. You can have a part in changing the landscape for the better.

After getting his start in real estate investments and building a standout reputation, Jeff learned of an opportunity to revive downtown Hartford, Connecticut. The city and state had targeted an area that had seen a loss of people and businesses and was on a mission to bring residents and companies back. The history of the city showed that at one time, it had been an insurance capital. "In the late 1980s there was an exodus of insurance companies . . . and then the residential population had started to move out," Jeff recalled.[4]

Jeff and his partner, who ran a well-known construction company, turned their sights to the area and started discussing possibilities. There were various signs that pointed to growth in the coming years. The state decided to consolidate its agencies to the downtown area. The University of Connecticut opted to move several of its campuses to the center of the city. Plans had been drawn up to build a minor league baseball stadium in Hartford too.

In addition, "the state set up an agency to fund multifamily downtown," Jeff shared. "We could see that growth was going to occur and we wanted to participate in it." To start, Jeff and his construction partner acquired a dilapidated hotel. "At one time, it was the iconic hotel in downtown Hartford," he noted. When Jeff came on the scene, it had been completely vacant for 15 years. The remembrances, however, were still alive. "We listened to stories and everyone who was middle-aged had a memory about a life event of theirs that occurred in the hotel, or some recollection of it," Jeff told the audience.[5]

Together with his partner, Jeff transformed the property from a 300-room hotel to 190 apartments. The process was far from simple. The purchase price was $500,000 for a building with a size of 200,000 square feet. This came to $2.50 a foot (as mentioned in Step 3, you'll often see properties priced by the square foot—and, I might add, this low figure initially looks like a steal! But there's more to the story).

Despite the low price, "we still couldn't make the economics work at first," Jeff lamented.[6] The renovation costs were just too high. When the partners investigated what they could receive in rent for the newly finished apartments, the figures didn't seem to cover the initial expenses.

What could be done? Jeff, who thrives in complicated transactions and believes his competitive advantage lies in the complexity of a deal, dug into the numbers. He leaned on his partner for construction knowledge, and the two brought in other experts to help, including an architect. While working with the architect, they decided to carry out a historic restoration to make the building appear as it did during its legendary days. The architect told the partners that tax credits were available for projects that created or renovated historic landmarks.

In addition, an inspection revealed that a significant amount of environmental remediation would have to be carried out, which meant the partners could receive money from the Department of Housing. A consultant came in to help with the government financing. They were able to secure funding from the state-established agency that aimed to invest in multifamily projects.

"We cobbled that all together," Jeff said. "It was a jigsaw puzzle."[7]

Once the contracts were signed, Jeff and his partner moved forward. They carried out the renovation and created a building that once again stood prominently in the center of Hartford. Then they watched tenants move in. "Now there are people constantly going into the building, and people are proud to see the building," he explained. "The exterior looks identical to what it looked like in 1962."[8]

While there were financial returns, the feeling of purpose perhaps surpassed those paper statements. "It's gratifying when you see a project you are involved in that has transformed a neighborhood," Jeff shared. "I can't go to Hartford without having at least one person say, 'Thank you for everything you've done.'"[9]

KEY TAKEAWAYS

- When it comes to managing the property, you'll need to consider whether you want to do it on your own or bring in a property manager.

- Value-add properties might require construction to put the new vision into place, and if you carry out the process well, these types of projects typically present the largest opportunities and returns.

- Revamping a community or neighborhood can bring returns and a sense of satisfaction, as you'll know you helped others and made a difference in their day-to-day lives.

STEP 9

Find the Right Tenants

True or false: when you have a tenant who is friendly and doesn't give you trouble, a handshake can take the place of a lease.

That statement is absolutely 100% false, according to Christina Smyth, a New York attorney and owner of Smyth Law, when she joined me on a panel discussion for my podcast.[1] Christina specializes in multifamily landlord and development counsel and trust me, she's seen a lot. "You need the four corners—a document to govern what goes on between the landlord and tenant," she shared.

Fair enough. At first glance, a lease might seem like a breeze of a step (especially compared to some of the others, like the mountain of paperwork you'll have to climb during the raising capital stage!). Signing a piece of paper can be done within a few seconds, but the terms that are locked in from that moment could make—or break—your return. A full lease document can run 150 pages—or more—depending on the conditions that are put into place.

Ample work should be carried out up front for a lease, and you'll want to make sure your timing is in order. When done well, a lease can be your ticket to getting those game-changing returns. You'll have all the clauses you need in place to protect your money, keep your investors, lenders, and partners happy, and provide a home for someone else or a place for a business in the meantime.

Residential leases are different from commercial leases. We'll break down each so you know how to handle them. After you gain an understanding of the components related to leasing, you'll be able to oversee tenants and create partnerships with them that can be mutually beneficial.

INSIDER TIP

Leases play an important role in the investment process, as they generate the bulk of your revenue from a property. Creating favorable ones for tenants can help you avoid the costs associated with filling empty units, as satisfied dwellers may be less likely to relocate. It will also help you navigate problems in the future.

ALL ABOUT RENT

In the lease agreement, the clauses will outline the relevant financial details related to the tenant and the space. "The most important clause is the rental clause," Christina mentioned.[2] The agreement will spell out how much the rent is, when it is due, and how it might change. For instance, there could be a rental increase year after year, or if you're in an area with rent regulation, there will be a cap listing the maximum amount of rent that can be charged. The timeframe for the lease, including how long it is valid, will be noted.

The lease will also lay out how expenses will be paid. Pass-through expenses refer to costs that the tenant will cover or help to cover. The utility bill might pass through to the tenant, for instance.

Or the renter might cover the property's taxes, insurance, or maintenance costs.

"There could be some concessions," Christina added.[3] These are perks that an owner or landlord offers to tenants in exchange for them coming on to the property and staying there. Let's say you're looking at buying a four-unit apartment building in a somewhat saturated market. It's vacant, and when you buy it, you need to bring in tenants. You might offer some incentives to get the place filled. Perhaps you decide to give each tenant two months of rent for free as a thank you for signing the lease. Those concessions could play out in several ways:

- The two months of free rent are given at the end of the calendar year, so nothing is paid during November and December.
- The two months of free rent are divided by 12; the amount is taken off each month's rent bill, which lowers the monthly payment.
- The tenant agrees to not pay the two months at the end of the lease; if they decide to move out, their last 60 days will be rent-free.

These concessions are beneficial for tenants, and they help an owner fill a place. If you're coming in as a buyer, however, bear in mind that these incentives may not appear front and center on a rent roll. You'll need to look through the fine print, which might consist of 2 pages of text or up to 18 to 20 pages (or more), depending on the market in your area.

INSIDER TIP

Tread carefully with concessions, as the best ones will be market-appropriate and still keep you in a strong financial position. Check what other investors are doing before you offer your own set of perks.

"If you see a rent concession rider, your net effective rent might be lower than the rent that's produced on the rent roll," Christina explained.[4] In other words, you won't receive the full potential of the rent roll. This will reduce the income you receive each month.

BUILDING IN PROTECTION

Push the pause button before tallying up the rent roll and concessions to calculate a quick return on the building.

"In a lease, you want utmost protection," Larry Haber, an experienced commercial real estate attorney and partner of the Commercial Real Estate Department of the bicoastal law firm Abrams Garfinkel Margolis Bergson, explained when he joined Christina and myself on my podcast.[5] "You're putting your money and your investors' money on the line, and signing a mortgage." The financial stakes are there: it's up to you and your team to do all you can to mitigate risks.

Rather than being scared away by these facts, consider the opportunities as well. "Make sure there is stable and secure cash flow," Larry suggested. "Cash flow is the oxygen you breathe." Here are three ways to get the money needle moving in the right direction:

Security deposit. A landlord or owner can ask a tenant for an amount up front to show their commitment to paying on time and caring for the property. While it's not a legal requirement, it tends to be standard practice in many areas. The maximum amount you can charge will vary from state to state and could range from one month of rent to more for an apartment.[6] You can also check how much other landlords are asking. These funds are typically deposited before the renter moves in. The agreement usually indicates that the money will be returned when the tenant moves out, assuming there isn't damage on the property or unpaid rent. On the other hand, if a tenant damages the property or stops paying, you can use those funds to cover the repairs and make up lost rental income.

Up-front rent. Instead of a security deposit, some landlords and owners will ask for an amount to pay for the last month of rent. Sometimes referred to as a nonrefundable security deposit, this amount is not expected to be returned to the tenant. Instead, you can agree to not charge the tenant for the final rent payment of their term.[7]

Lease guarantee. This can be used for residential and commercial spaces, though the specific agreements will differ. For residential, the guarantee is an agreement that is signed by the landlord, tenant, and a third party who meets the financial requirements.[8] The third party assumes responsibility for any tenant defaults, agreeing to cover missed rent payments and anything else outlined in the lease terms.

Think of a college student who graduates and rents their first apartment in a big city. The young person might not have a lengthy credit history or padded savings account. The parents, however, have an ample stash in their retirement portfolio and a long record of solid credit. They could come on as a guarantor and agree to cover rent payments should the new graduate lose their job or get in a financial bind. This saves you, the investor, the anxiety that can come from worrying about whether rent will show up month after month.

For commercial, the arrangement is made with a third party, which is often a creditworthy business related to the tenant. On the podcast, Larry called out this setup, which in New York City is commonly called a "Good Guy Guarantee."

The concept (which applies in other regions, though the exact name may be different) is that a "good guy" will agree to cover any rent obligations under the lease if the tenant moves out before the term ends. These are often arranged for businesses, such as a franchisee who comes in and has the parent corporation agree to guarantee the lease. If the franchisee decides to vacate the spot prematurely, the corporation will provide the landlord with sufficient notice, as laid out in the terms of the lease. The corporation will cover all rent expenses up to the time the tenant leaves, and deliver the property in broom-clean condition, with all belongings and garbage removed from the site.[9]

DUE DILIGENCE FOR TENANTS

Who should you bring on as a tenant? Good question. Just as you carry out due diligence for a property before acquiring it, you'll want to evaluate your renters—preferably before they arrive with their bags and boxes, ready to settle in! This review process varies, depending on the type of space you have. We'll look at how to handle both residential tenants and commercial ones.

Residential tenants. Rule number one: don't "go with your gut." While we'd love to take on everybody in good faith, remember that you likely have lenders, a partner, and some other investors all planning to get their share in the deal. They'll expect a vetting process, and quite honestly, you'll be better off knowing that your tenants meet the financial requirements to pay rent and use the place in a fair way.

This process can start with an application which asks for information about:

- **Current and previous employers.** You could request data from the past three to five years, including how long the tenant stayed at each job.
- **Income level.** You want to see that they can cover their rent and living expenses. Some places use a requirement such as the "40 Times Rent Rule," which means the tenant should have an annual salary that is at least 40 times the monthly rent. Following this guideline, if a lease is set for $2,000 a month, the tenant should earn at least $80,000 a year (40 × $2,000).[10] Another industry standard consists of the 30% threshold. With this, you would ask tenants to spend up to

30% (but not over) of their income on rent. A person making $5,000 a month could look at a maximum rent of $1,500.[11]

- **Past renting experiences.** You might have potential tenants share where they previously lived, how much they paid in rent, and why they left.
- **Personal references.** You could ask the applicant to send over the names and contact information for a few friends and family members who can vouch for their character.

You might also opt to run a credit check to see if any past debts, bankruptcies, or other credit pitfalls appear. In some cases, an interview could be helpful to see the tenant in person and understand their situation. A leasing agent can help with these steps, though it's good for investors to know the process being taken for each property.

Commercial tenants. You'll sleep better at night if you have a thorough sense that the business renting your property is financially sound. It's common to ask for financial statements from a commercial client, including:

- Up to two years' worth of taxes, balance sheets, and profit and loss statements
- Personal financial statements
- Business bank statements[12]

In addition, you can request to see a business plan and run credit checks on the individuals leading the company. Looking at the company's rental history can also clue you in to how they'll perform in your space. How long were they at their last location? Why did they leave? The exact questions you ask and information you gather will depend on the tenant and the location. For instance, if the property can easily be leased to other businesses, the due diligence process might be simple. A place that you've specifically customized for a tenant will likely require a more thorough investigation; after all, you want to start getting—and continuing to receive—a return on your investment.

PARTNERING CREATES A WIN-WIN

There are so many nuances that come up from the beginning of the lease process to the end of the tenant's stay. Some of these are easy to see: Did the rent check arrive? Did the tenant renew the lease? Are most of the units filled? Other issues, however, are much grayer, and yet are of equal or greater importance.

As you work through each detail, keep in mind that a happy tenant that stays is often your best-case scenario. (This is assuming the rents are at market rates and the tenant is paying on time.) Given this, you may work out arrangements to keep them satisfied and save you the trouble of having to find a new tenant. Here are a few considerations to keep in mind as you build a relationship with tenants.

An Understanding of Responsibility

Who will pay for what? In a retail space, the tenant might cover the utilities they use. In an apartment building, you may absorb those costs. When dividing up expenses, keep in mind that if tenants feel short-changed, they might look for a different place. Rather than trying to load as many operating costs as possible to the renter, aim to make it a two-way street. Perhaps they cover utilities while you'll oversee the repairs and maintenance of the place.

Creating the Right Space

When you have a tenant who wants to change the property to fit their needs, it may be best to strike up a conversation. Perhaps a business arrives to the property and needs a workplace that meets specific criteria, including conference rooms designed in a certain way. You might agree to deliver the property as a turnkey solution, meaning it's ready for the tenant to move in and use. Or you could discuss the consequences of the tenant overseeing the improvements. In such a case, you might offer to lower the rent to make it easier, cost-wise, for the tenant to renovate.

Room to Grow

In some situations, there may be opportunities to set rent at a certain floor, along with a tied percentage based on earnings. Here's how it works: Suppose you have a restaurant come into a place and agree to pay $7,000 every month. In addition, the eatery will pay 10% of their sales to you. You know that no matter how the business performs, you'll receive a check for seven grand each pay period. If the restaurant sells $50,000 each month, you'll get an additional $5,000 (0.10 × $50,000). These agreements can create a dual benefit for everyone; the restaurant can better manage its expenses and as sales increase, so will your rent roll.

INSIDER TIP

Look to build partnerships with your tenants and don't be afraid to go above and beyond your competitors in the way you treat them. Residents will notice and it could attract additional tenants.

For one of my first investments, I purchased a three-family apartment building in Cold Spring, New York. My wife and I were living in New York City at the time and wanted to use the place as a getaway on the weekends. We fixed the property up and then rented out the two apartments we weren't using to tenants. The process helped me learn a lot about tenants and leases.

Overall, the experience was excellent: I kept the units in optimal condition and the tenants were satisfied. There were few complaints and a sense of all-around appreciation. I eventually sold the place, but the time with those tenants taught me the value of creating a partnership. If you cultivate great relationships with your tenants, just as you do with your other team members, the potential for mutual wins is high. All it takes is an understanding of the lease process and an eagerness to reach out a hand when needed.

KEY TAKEAWAYS

- The details related to rent, increase, pass-through expenses, and the term are the most important components of a lease, as they will dictate the financial performance of your investment.

- Build in financial protection by adding terms in the lease related to a security deposit, up-front rent, or a guarantor who can vouch for the tenant.

- Due diligence for residential tenants might include a check on their current and past employers, income level, past renting experiences, and a list of references. For commercial tenants, the process could call for tax returns, balance sheets, profit and loss statements, personal financial statements, and bank account information. To vet a tenant, call their references, including their current and previous landlords.

- For financial provisions with commercial tenants, pay attention to the increases over time. Also look at the tenant's contribution toward taxes. Typically, tenants will reimburse for a portion of the real estate tax increase as well as their own utility consumption.

- Divide up expenses fairly, keep properties in above-average condition compared to competitors, and create flexibility to allow tenants to thrive and even grow if they so choose.

STEP 10

Reap the Rewards

As Francis Greenburger, an entrepreneur, real estate developer, and philanthropist who has made a significant contribution to both New York's landscape and nonprofits, began his investment journey, he treaded slowly. He discovered the opportunities in real estate investing almost by accident. At the time, he needed office space for a small company he was running that catered to the publishing industry. He found a property with two offices for lease. "I only need one," he told the landlord. "That's fine," was the reply. "Rent both and sublet the other one."[1]

Francis did just that, and brought in enough from his tenant to cover the rent for both offices. His eyes had been opened, and when another opportunity came up, he plunged in. This time, he noticed that the codes were changing. Rent regulation had been in effect for years, and led to owners having to charge such low rents that they couldn't afford to keep their buildings operating. Enter deregulation, and the chance for owners to raise the rent after the tenants moved out.

Francis found a run-down building listed for a low price, as the owner had been charging regulated rents for years to the tenants and

177

didn't think it was worth much. Francis, on the other hand, figured he could fix up the units and rent them for more once the tenants changed over.[2]

He had a great idea—and little cash—so he presented the concept to a couple of potential partners. They loved his business plan and brought him in with sweat equity. The project proved to be all Francis expected—and more. The returns were so substantial that he went on to invest in other properties.[3]

As the trends evolved, Francis continued to discover ways to do things that were a bit out of the norm—but he had positive results. When the codes changed again, sweeping in a revival movement to switch rental housing to co-op ownership, Francis jumped in. He spotted a 40-unit apartment building for sale for $1 million. The owner had rented the spaces for years and wanted the $1 million to fund his retirement. Francis agreed to the price but asked if he could stretch the closing. In effect, he wanted to pay the owner bit by bit, offering a little more than $25,000 for each apartment . . . when he sold it. The owner agreed, and Francis went out to sell the units. The first one he sold brought in $500,000. He paid the owner the $25,000-plus, as agreed, and moved on to sell the others.[4]

Francis went on to even bigger and better deals—and that's exactly what this chapter is about. While the journey you follow will be your own, like Francis you can uplevel your game and add to your real estate portfolio. After you've acquired a property, carried out necessary renovations, leased it, and started generating a cash flow, it's time to make another decision. Should you hold the place? Refinance to get better loan terms? Sell?

Your business plan, along with the expectations of the partners and investors involved, will play a large role guiding your decision. The same can be said for market trends like interest rates and job growth. Let's lay out the different options available, starting with holding the property and then moving on to refinancing and selling.

> **INSIDER TIP**
>
> Your business plan is a key tool to attract like-minded investors.
> It should spell out the life of the investment and how it will
> ultimately be capitalized. Optionality is also key if you need
> more time to complete the business plan or even buy out your
> partners in the future.

THE INS AND OUTS OF HOLDING

If you purchase a four-unit apartment building and live in one of the units, you could be on your way to generating cash from the other three units. After several years, while enjoying passive income from the property, you might be ready to reside in a different place. Whether you keep the building will depend on your finances and goals. Perhaps you can sell and get a new deal in the area where you'll be moving. Maybe you want to hang on to the place and use other funds to make another investment.

If there are more team players, such as a partner and other investors involved in the deal, you'll have additional layers to consider. In the investing world, the time you keep a place will often be directed by the agreements you have with your partner and other investors. Sometimes a person who contributes as an investor to a deal will want to be involved for five to seven years, and then they'll be ready to move on. They will look for their preferred return and thank you for the investment opportunity. Then they'll shift their funds elsewhere.

When this happens, it means you'll need to find a way to continue financing the property on your own or with your partner. You might be able to refinance or bring on other investors. If you can't make it work to continue getting a return, or if the market takes a dip, you could find yourself putting up a "For Sale" sign when the investors leave.

THE ART OF REFINANCING

When you first take out a loan for a property, you may have higher interest rates for several reasons. Banks charge more for loans that are not made on primary residences, as they assume if finances get tight you'll pay the mortgage on your main home first and, only after that, the investment property. You might have secured a bridge loan, which acts as a temporary source of funding and will have higher rates than other types of loans. If there is construction involved, the debt is usually more expensive—plus you might have to personally guarantee the loan.

Once any construction is complete, or you've paid off some of the principal loan amount, your mortgage broker can look into permanent financing. These loans are more attractive than bridge loans and construction loans, as they'll often provide lower interest rates and better terms. As a result, you could end up with higher cash flow from the property.

The main reasons to refinance include:

- Getting a lower interest rate
- Lengthening the term of the loan to reduce payments
- Getting cash out to re-invest or use for other projects

Suppose you have a 10-year loan on a property which has a variable interest rate that is currently at 8%. Perhaps you can refinance to get a 20-year loan with a fixed interest rate of 5%. This move will lower your monthly payments and give you a longer period of time to pay off the loan.

Lenders will have different requirements when it comes to how much equity you'll need to have to be eligible for a refinance. Many want to see a loan-to-value ratio that is lower than 75%, meaning you'd have 25% or more equity in the building. For a property that is appraised at $1,000,000 with a $600,000 mortgage, the loan-to-value ratio will be 60% ($600,000 / $1,000,000). Your equity will be $400,000, which comes to 40% ($400,000 / $1,000,000). You could tap into this equity and get better terms on the loan through a refinance.

Ideally, you'll do a refinance that gives all the partners and investors the equity they initially put into the deal. In this case, your returns will be infinite. You can take the proceeds and go buy another property.

> ## INSIDER TIP
>
> Have your mortgage broker put the best terms on the table beyond just rate and proceeds. You want to carefully consider the length on your loan and any guarantees that you could be asked to make. Loan provisions can differ greatly depending on the profile of the lender.

SHOULD YOU SELL?

If a refinance can't get you enough cash to receive your desired return, you might think about selling. If you do, there could be taxes involved with the transaction. In real estate, if you sell a property that you've had as an investment, you could face the capital gains tax. This category is divided into short-term capital gains tax and long-term capital gains tax. Let's look at both:

Short-term capital gains tax. If you purchase a property and sell it within the same year, you'll pay a tax rate on the gains that is the same as your income tax rate.[5] Suppose you buy a place for $100,000 and sell it six months later for $150,000. The $50,000 increase ($150,000 − $100,000) will be subject to your income tax rate. If you're in the 24% bracket, you'll pay $12,000 in taxes for the sale (0.24 × $50,000).[6]

Long-term capital gains tax. Holding a property for longer than a year will mean that when you sell, it could be subject to a different tax rate. Under the long-term capital gains tax, depending on your income (and the ever-shifting tax codes) you might have to pay 15% to 20% of the profits earned to the IRS.[7] Following with the example of purchasing a home for $100,000, if you sell it five years later for $150,000, the $50,000 gain will face a long-term capital gains tax. If you're in the 24% tax bracket for your income, you'll have to pay a 15% tax rate on the $50,000. The IRS bill would be $7,500 (0.15 × $50,000).

Initially, that long-term capital gains tax might look better than the shorter one, but if you dig a little deeper, you'll find many investors aren't excited about the longer tax terms either. They might see it as a cut into their return, which is why when a sale takes place in my line of work, I often hear the term "1031 exchange" get tossed around. Let's look at that next.

1031 EXCHANGE EXPLAINED

Named for Section 1031 of the IRS tax code, this provision allows you to swap one investment property for another without having to pay the capital gains tax. The code is based on the idea that income is taxed, and if no income is created, there isn't a tax tied to it. That said, there are many rules revolving around this code, so you'll need to tread carefully and lean on experts to walk you through. Here are a few factors to keep in mind along the way.

It's Applicable to Similar Properties

Your next purchase will have to be "like-kind," meaning it will need to be comparable in nature, though it doesn't have to be an exact swap. The equity and debt of the new property must be the same or greater than the one sold if you wish to defer the full capital gains tax. The acquisition will need to be another investment, so a home you'll live in or a vacation home you want to have for solely personal use will not qualify.

You'll Need an Intermediary

Also known as an exchange facilitator or qualified intermediary (QI), this entity will hold your funds in escrow, which is a legal arrangement that involves a third party temporarily holding your money until the next purchase agreement is completed. This third party could be a person or company. It's important to vet the intermediary so you don't end up missing a few requirements and paying taxes on the gain right away. Ask these questions when looking for the right third party to hold your funds in escrow:

- Do you have experience with 1031 exchanges and real estate?
- Are you compliant and up-to-date with the annual examinations the IRS issues?
- Can you provide a view to my money at all times?
- Will the funds be held in an FDIC-insured dual signature account? This means that both you and the QI will have to sign off to transfer the funds into a new investment.

Timing Is Everything

You'll have 45 days after your first property sells to find up to three potential replacement properties. (If you find more than three, there will be additional requirements to work through. This practice falls under the 200% rule, meaning that the total properties identified can't be worth more than twice the amount for which your property sold.) You'll put these finds in writing and share it with the seller or the qualified intermediary. You'll then need to close on the next property (or properties) within 180 days of closing on the first property.

If you don't use all the gains from your first sale toward the second, you can expect to pay a tax on what remains, which is called the boot. The same is true if you miss other rules related to the 1031 exchange, which is why working with a qualified professional will be helpful. Ask your partner for a reference and think about a long-term plan before making any moves. Before you sell the first property, you should have an idea of what you want to buy next, or a path that will help you meet the timeline requirements. When negotiating, you can work in terms related to the 1031 exchange, such as asking the buyer to wait to close until you are ready to move forward on the next properties.

INSIDER TIP

While the 1031 exchange may seem like a great way to trade up into your next investment, never buy a property for tax reasons alone. A purchase must always stand on its own.

THE RIGHT BROKER

When it's time to sell, you should look for a broker who exclusively works on the sell side. This broker will represent you to the market and aim to get the highest sales price possible. You'll have the broker first value your property and share their estimate.

As you choose a selling broker, look for these traits:

A solid marketing strategy. Will the listing be posted on multiple sites such as CoStar, Loopnet, Crexi, and Property IDX? Will they work with the whole brokerage community and share fees 50/50? Do they have a strong social media presence to leverage?

A great track record. What have they sold in the past? What sets their experiences apart from others? In what areas do they specialize? Do they have a great team to provide support?

A tangible timeline. How long will this take? What are the market conditions?

A good broker will bring you multiple offers. If you get a strong first bid, there may be initial excitement. It's hard to make a decision in a vacuum, though. You won't have other options to compare, which is why waiting to get more offers can work in your favor. When you enter the negotiating contract, you can look for the highest bidder with the best terms.

These steps are the start of what could be a long-term portfolio. You might decide to refinance and hold the property, or you could opt to sell and carry out a 1031 exchange to continue along the investment path. The second time around, you'll be able to draw on your initial meetings, paperwork, deals, and list of contacts to build up. You might specialize in one asset class or diversify. It's up to you, and the only limit is your imagination. Let the creativity flow and you'll be well-prepared for success.

KEY TAKEAWAYS

- For investors who hold properties for an extended period, there could come a time when refinancing provides the chance to get more favorable terms and payment conditions.

- After you've increased cash flows to a property, a refinance could result in a "cash out" refi. In some cases, successful investors are able to pull out all their equity. If this happens, your returns will be infinite!

- To defer capital gains taxes when selling, some investors opt for a 1031 exchange, which allows you to sell an investment and shift the proceeds into like kind properties.

- When selling, look for an investment sales broker who has a strong record selling your product in your neighborhood. Hear their plan on how they will maximize the exposure of your property and reach as many buyers as possible. Look for a broker's opinion of value and justify their recommended pricing by referencing other comparable sales. Make sure the broker will cooperate and share fees with buyer brokers too.

BONUS STEP
Create Your Dream Team

D o you want to go far in real estate investing? (I'm guessing "yes," since you've read up to this point!) We've discussed how success stems from surrounding yourself with the right people. Keep in mind, however, that you don't have to build up an entire team that includes every single person mentioned in the previous pages to get started with real estate investing. When you're fresh to this game, it takes time to build relationships, and I'm not suggesting you spend years cultivating bonds before attempting your first bid.

The key here, as entrepreneur Don Peebles shared on my podcast, is "getting into the mix of real estate." As head of Peebles Corporation, a privately held real estate investment and development company, Don has followed that strategy from early on. In high school, he served as a congressional page in Washington, DC, and started to make political connections.[1]

He drew on relationships again in his early twenties, when he formed an appraisal business in the country's capital. He really wanted to be a developer at that time, so he let people in his network know of the interest. In response, a broker presented him a development opportunity that changed the trajectory of his career. Today, Peebles Corporation engages in affirmative development and has realized real estate development through public-private partnerships in major US cities. The firm has a portfolio of active and completed developments that total more than 10 million square feet and $8 billion. (And to think, it all started by "getting into the mix," which is exactly what this chapter is about!)[2]

To be clear, these are team members you should bring into your fold in a natural way. You don't have to go and retain an attorney, who might start billing hours for long conversations about possibilities. In such a case, you could end up paying for a legal service before you've even found an opportunity. Rather, there are many ways to make connections and they almost always include a bit of give-and-take, and not many (if any) fees to start. Let's go over some of these and I think you'll agree with me when I say that this is where the magic begins—and how you can make new friends along the way.

INSIDER TIP

The stronger your relationships with service providers, the better. They can also be a great source for deals and introductions to potential partners and investors.

Attend Industry Events

Check your local listings for upcoming conferences, trade shows, panels, summits, and other events related to real estate. I go to many of these gatherings, including events put on by Bisnow, GreenPearl, the International Council of Shopping Centers (ICSC), and the National Multifamily Housing Council (NMHC). When I attend, I learn a lot about the market and what's going on in my area. These gatherings create a perfect chance to meet other people involved in transactions, talk to them about what they're doing, and ask questions. If I run into an attorney at one of these, I might casually pose, "What are you working on? How can I be helpful?" The same with accountants, to whom I may inquire, "What's keeping you up at night? How are you advising your clients these days? Are there ways I can be of assistance?" Now, certainly I don't give accounting or legal advice, but the conversation leads to an opening of doors that helps me understand what the opportunities are in the market, and how I might connect with the right people to secure them.

Join Alliances

I helped cofound RESA (Real Estate Services Alliance), an organization based in New York City that consists of top-level professionals involved in various aspects of the industry. Its members participate in fields spanning the gamut from brokerage services to management, marketing, transactional, architectural design, construction, lending, and more. Owners and others who need real estate services can browse the membership listings and find reputable sources whom they can reach out to and ask for a consultation.

There may be alliances or real estate–minded organizations in your area. There are also professional designations such as CCIM, which stands for Certified Commercial Investment Member. If you enroll to receive this designation, you'll learn about the fundamentals of underwriting and will also get access to a great network. Search online or follow the social media pages of well-known real estate professionals in your city. When you meet with a broker, ask if they recommend joining any local organizations.

Start Small

Please don't think that you can't move forward in a deal before you develop a team of 20 players, all ready to get involved in a real estate bid. Far from it. The good news is that once you have a couple of contacts who are really plugged in, they'll help make introductions to other professionals. If I had someone who was looking to invest in New York and they needed some recommendations for a title agent, tax attorney, or mortgage broker, I definitely have some suggestions I could make.

When you're new in this line of investing, zero in on finding just one of these professionals to explore a partnership with for your first deal. Invite that person out for coffee and talk to them to understand their business. If that person has years of experience purchasing and selling properties, they likely know others in the space, and more precisely, have opinions about who they *prefer* to be involved in their transactions and projects. Cream rises to the top, as they say, and high-performing individuals tend to become known in this space— and often for good reason. They're smart, know how to add value, and might just be looking to build their network too. You likely have something to offer them, and vice versa. Once you have the chance to meet a few individuals, you can look at taking it to the next level and meeting more, and so on.

INSIDER TIP

When highly regarded professionals speak, listen carefully to glean information that goes beyond the norm. By asking follow-up questions, you might uncover inside information that other investors won't pick up on—simply because they are hyper focused on their own ideas and not as open to input from other sources.

Value Every Relationship

Suppose you make a list of all the team players you'll need. You note all the names we've covered so far. Then you head out and start meeting people. You come across a tenant-landlord broker, who you meet through your partner. You learn the tenant-landlord broker's name is Joe, and he has a great reputation. Now, should you go back to your list of people you need to meet and cross off "tenant-landlord broker?"

Not necessarily. In networking, I like to think the more the merrier. Building relationships far and wide will give you ample opportunities to gain inside information that isn't readily available through public channels. It also serves a practical purpose. Some of these professionals get so specialized that you may want to work with one type of tenant-landlord broker for one property, and a different one for another building.

There's also some benefit in having an extensive network to match up your side with that of the seller. You might be looking at a piece of property and see that the seller brings in a team of lawyers from a big-name law firm. To balance this, you may decide to hire the same type of team to carry out the transaction. On the other hand, if the seller has a single attorney taking care of everything, you could also decide to contract a smaller law firm for the related paperwork.

Leverage Referrals

The best relationships tend to stand out against the rest as a continuum of good rapport, strong communication, and progress for both sides. I'm generally quick to share helpful information with everyone from my client base to students who are learning the trade, and anyone in between. I've found that being generous with what you have to offer will come back to you in a good way.

I can't tell you the number of times I've had someone call me and say, "James, I just spoke to someone who said they're friends with you, and we're looking to sell our property. They recommended I reach out to you." When I get a referral such as this, I take it very, very seriously. I recognize that the person—in this example, my friend—has put their own name on the line by referring me. I know I need to deliver, and more than that, I want to go out of my way to make sure the client is well taken care of. There are a lot of referrals in real estate, and they create an opportunity to strengthen relationships—and generate more business.

Don't Focus on Fees

As I mentioned in Step 2, some professionals in the real estate world will charge hourly rates; others are success based and will earn a commission when the transaction takes place. Some will come with a set service fee or retainer, which is usually paid up front and covers a specific time or case. As you get to know these individuals and meet with them, you'll see a variety of fees—some lower than others and some on the very high end. Like other industries, you might come across a professional that charges one rate and another professional in the same line of work that charges double or triple for the same services.

I know from experience that when starting out it can be easy to feel a tug toward lower prices. There's a certain reasoning to this approach; if we're making an investment, the less we pay at the beginning, the higher the return at the end. However, I often tell people that this isn't always the case. In real estate, you often get what you pay for.

Suppose you're going to carry out an exciting development project. You want to purchase a piece of property you've been eyeing. It's been marketed as a great spot to build a 50,000-square-foot structure. You know you need a land use attorney to help figure out what can legally be done on the property. When you look through your contact list of land use attorneys, you see that you have two in your network. With a little research, you learn that one of them charges an hourly fee that is double the other one. Should you opt for the cheaper one?

Following my logic that you may need to pay for the best professional in the space, let's say you reach out to the more expensive one. This land use attorney has an all-star reputation, and you know they've done a lot of projects before like the one you're taking on. You sit down with this highly rated and pricey land use attorney and they agree to take a look at the project. Shortly after meeting, they call you and say they believe they could get the property upzoned, which means to change the zoning codes to allow for a higher or more dense building. Rather than putting up a 50,000-square-foot building as you had first envisioned, and as it had been advertised, the land use attorney says you could double the square footage.

Now that's a game-changing component. Suddenly you can create a building that is twice as large as originally suggested. Think of the additional rents that could bring, all from the same amount of land. Sure, you will have to pay more for this land use attorney with the higher hourly rate, but by opting for them, they've helped you unlock additional value. What if you had gone with the lower-priced land use attorney? They might not have been able to secure this variance, and while you would have paid a lower lawyer fee, you'd have only received a 50,000-square-foot building at the end of the day.

INSIDER TIP

There's an adage, "You get what you pay for." The right professionals can save you a ton of time and money in the long run and avoid costly mistakes. That said, you need to budget your soft costs going into a transaction. You don't want to get in over your head on a deal if the costs to bring on the right team are too much.

It's not always crystal clear to sort through the different rates and find those individuals who will add true value. When deciding who to contact, you can look at their track record and experience. Those who have substantial time in the industry might charge more, but they may be able to carry out the same tasks in less time, because they've done it so many times before. In this case, you could end up paying nearly the same amount for a less experienced person who charges lower fees per hour but takes longer to carry out the services as you would pay someone with years in the trade who doesn't need as much time. Professionals with standout projects in the past who have been in their business for a long time will often be the top of the stack in terms of the value they can add to a project.

That said, if your property and business plan are small and simple, you might not need those top-notch, loophole-finding services. Instead, a lower-priced or less experienced professional might get the job done well. It comes down to evaluating what you need, researching what's available, and not being afraid to pay more for professionals who can add significant value if the project calls for it.

Align Yourself with Integrity

The professionals you retain, and those who join you for a breakfast meeting or building tour, serve as a bit of a mirror. They show a reflection of who you are in the real estate world.

As you start to build your connections, it might seem like there are so many people out there that if you bend a few rules, or make an unethical decision, you'll go unnoticed. That's not the case. People talk. Consider my own location in New York City, which is filled with almost 9 million people.[3] There's more than 1 million buildings in the metro area.[4] Surely it would seem that if I cut corners on a deal, no one would find out. Not so. If I carry out business that doesn't run by the books, others will take note. Remember that nearly every transaction in real estate investing involves a team of players, so there will be others sitting at the table when we close who can either see—or may learn later when they do a little research—that I cut corners along the way.

Building your real estate investment portfolio in a respectable, law-abiding way is certainly the right thing to do. In addition, when we take a long-term view, we see that it is the best way to add value. If others learn about the deal in which I cut corners, will they want to work with me again? (Especially if they lost something in the deal?) They won't see me as trustworthy. My reputation, just like yours, is on the line every time I come to the table to negotiate a deal. It's also there when I pick up the phone, walk the streets, and meet up with others.

When I work with a client, I always try to put myself in their shoes. I listen to what they are looking for and think about what's best for them. It's not unusual for me to have someone approach me and say, "James, I have this property that I'm considering putting up for sale. What do you think? Is now a good time?" If, based on my knowledge of the market, I don't think that the moment is best for them, I'll say so. I might be out a commission, as I'm advising them against a sale and I won't receive any fees for my chat about waiting. However, if I feel a certain way, I'll share my honest opinion.

Others looking for a quick sale and commission might advise that same client to sell and sell fast. If I see that they could probably get a better price by waiting a year, because I think properties like theirs will grow in value, I'm going to say, "Let's wait." If that client holds off, they might come to me the following year, simply because they trust me for my transparency.

INSIDER TIP

In real estate, a clean reputation—and being surrounded by credible people—is everything. Keep your head up during rough times and do the right thing, and others will notice.

As you get to know individuals, recognize that reputation doesn't only revolve around deals that went smoothly. Sometimes things happen that are beyond our control. During the financial crisis of 2009, I watched a lot of clients go through rough times, including those with built-up credibility.

Even if you're the best investor with the highest reputation, if the market changes, events could happen that are out of your control. Consider how people act during those unfortunate seasons. The individuals who continue to carry through with integrity, even in tough times, are the players you want on your team.

Here's the ultimate benefit: building up a strong reputation and credibility will bring in future value. You might have others reach out to you, based merely on your integrity and track record in the real estate world. Referrals often come to me this way. I work with someone on a deal, and they see the authenticity of my team members who are involved in the transaction. When their friend wants to invest, they send them to me. More business, more relationships, more value—and it all starts with building a network of other credible individuals who, like yourself, aim for integrity at every step.

Pay It Forward

It's so easy to think of networking as handing out a stack of business cards, working a room, or reaching out on LinkedIn to rack up your connections. While these can be effective strategies, when I meet others, I like to avoid looking like I am solely interested in advancing my own business. This somewhat counterintuitive approach is exactly what my good friend Jeff Meshel wrote about in his book, *One Phone Call Away*.[5] Jeff is a master networker and has more than 5,000 names in his Rolodex. He advises that the best way to reach out to others is to pick up the phone, start a conversation, and ask, "How can I help you?" When you give something of yourself to others, they appreciate it. And they'll think of you later when they have something to offer you.

Translating this to the real estate world, you might refer a seller to a broker you know, or you might share a trend you learned about with an attorney. I always see it as a two-way street. There are ample opportunities to listen to what others need and help them with a skill or knowledge you have. When you need assistance, they'll be some of the first people to answer your call.

THE BENEFITS OF REPEAT BUSINESS

Let's fast forward in time 10 years and say you're about to make your tenth real estate investment. (Congratulations! I'm hopeful the tips from this book helped you get off to the right start.) You want to get some acquisition financing, which refers to the funding an entity uses to obtain another entity. Rather than searching online for a mortgage broker, you reach out to the same person you've dealt with for loans for the last four deals. This broker has all the information about your past financing and nearly all the financial records needed to get started on the transaction. As you move through the process, everything goes smoothly and swiftly. Compare this to when you work with a mortgage broker for the first time, and they ask you for so many documents that you wonder when they are going to request your fourth-grade report card. The advantage here comes in the form of time saved.

There's also a level of bonding that repeat business brings. Suppose you call in the same team to help you put together a bid, and you all have worked together on two projects in the past. Chances are that during this third project, the feeling of camaraderie will grow even more. You'll have additional layers of trust, so when you face issues and obstacles along the way, it can be easier to come to a solution together.

Not long ago I was texting with my friend Jeff Ravetz, principal of Girona Ventures, about a multifamily project that he was bidding on. I've known Jeff for some time and have interviewed him on my podcast.[6] When we were sending messages back and forth about the project, he shared some sage words about the perks of working with the same professionals over time.

You see, Jeff has been involved in the business of real estate investing since his early days, when he visited properties on Long Island with his father. His agency has a track record of acquiring commercial properties that are performing below average and transforming them into top-notch spaces that retain high occupancy. In short, Jeff knows how to take properties that aren't doing well and make them beautiful . . . and then fill them with renters. For many of these projects, there are lenders involved. Jeff once said in a class he was teaching at NYU, "When you talk about relationships, lenders are really important. Even if you're using a mortgage broker to help you negotiate the terms, having that go-to lender who knows you as a borrower has comfort."

Jeff has certainly done his share of deals, and he was referring to lenders he has used time and again. He was remembering how hard that first piece of business can be in this industry. Part of the reason it's so tough is that you need to persuade others to have a general confidence in you and the project. You want everyone involved to believe your plans will indeed come through and you'll fulfill terms—or better.

Once you've made it over those initial hurdles and you have a success story to share . . . others notice. They pay attention to you next time you turn to them for assistance. The lender will see that you got the deal, delivered what you said you would, and paid the bank as planned. If you come to them again, they'll generally be more open to working with you. That sort of comfort is hard to measure in numbers, but, like Jeff mused, it's a great advantage to have.

There's a final plus to doing business again and again with the same people. When I spoke with Robert Rivani for my podcast, who by the way has closed more than $500 million since 2014, he emphasized the benefits of using the same team for multiple transactions.[7]

Robert founded Black Lion Investment Group in 2014 and shared with listeners his strategies for trading up. He thrives on buying properties, improving them, and selling them. Then he repeats that cycle again and again. He depends on a team that can manage the volume. They're quick to keep cranking through the deals, the upgrades, the sales, and then getting ready to start the cycle again. Imagine if he had to build up a team from scratch every time he spotted a property he was keen on fixing up. If you're like me, you're thinking he probably wouldn't have accrued half a billion dollars of transactions in a few short years without that A-team in place and running.

THE VALUE OF THE RIGHT TEAM

Quick question: How far can standout players at your side take you?

Answer: The possibilities abound. When I interviewed David Shorenstein, the principal and cofounder of Hildreth Real Estate Advisors, he shared incredible insights on what a high-performing team can accomplish.[8]

David has been in real estate for more than 15 years and accumulated a portfolio valued at more than $300 million with over 250 properties. Along the way, he created a team that included interns, who would draft handwritten letters to owners. These letters would ask if the owners were interested in selling their property and if so, suggest that they reach out to David's firm. There's no way David could have sat in his office by himself and written out every single one of those letters. He wouldn't have had the bandwidth! With a high-performing team of letter writers, however, those mailings could get sent out, and the prospective sellers would call in.

As I reflect on my own career, I recognize there's no way I could have reached the level that I have without a team surrounding me. When people ask me what I'm proud of, I always answer that it's not my personal success as a broker. I'm most proud of my team and the culture we've created. It's absolutely essential, and I wouldn't be here today without them.

Now let's think of you as a starting investor, and how the value can be found in the right team. Drawing on our previous example of building "live-work apartments," let's say you're the one who comes up with this idea. You carry out some initial research and ask around and find there is truly demand for this in your region. The thought gives you such a thrill that it keeps you up at night.

You head out on the streets and tap those in your network to seek out opportune properties. You find a well-structured loft building with the help of a broker. At first glance, it seems perfect. You immediately see ways to build in office space and still have separate living areas for tenants.

As a next step, you decide to make a business plan. This document will lay out what you have in mind, some basics on what it will cost, how it will operate, and how it will perform. As you're writing up the plan, you begin to think through the details related to the project. For starters, you wonder, what zoning and certificate of occupancy does this building I'm interested in have? Offices usually have their own zoning and code requirements, which are typically distinct from residential necessities. You worry about whether you can make changes and legally put in workplaces on a residential property.

Here is your opportunity to reach out to a member of your team and ask for help. In this case, you want an attorney who understands how zoning codes might work in your project, such as a land use attorney. If you're going to be building and selling apartments, you might also reach out to a condo attorney. Perhaps you talk to these individuals and bounce the idea off them. If you've built a relationship beforehand, and come across as credible, they'll very likely take your idea seriously.

You can openly ask about what obstacles they foresee with your plan and if they have recommendations on how to improve the project. Now, they might love the idea and point you in the right direction regarding zoning codes (during the discussion with the land use attorney) and how you might position these office/home apartments (from the condo attorney). Based on their areas of expertise, they could point out potential roadblocks and how to get over them. They might also say, "I love the idea . . . but have you thought of doing it in a different area?" Maybe the land use attorney knows the best place to develop this based on their inside knowledge of the zoning codes. Or the condo attorney may be aware of a different neighborhood where downtown dwellers are moving. You could then start looking at property options there.

Even if you don't know the attorney very well, or don't know an attorney at all, reach out to get started, and you'll likely receive a free hour-long consultation. This is generally part of their practice, and they view it as meeting with a prospective partner or client. During the session, they'll typically readily share advice, which you can soak up (don't forget to take notes!). This information is usually given with the expectation that if you like what you hear, there may be an opportunity to work together, in which case both parties win. Again, it's okay to not have the entire team built up at once. The game-changing factor is that you're reaching out and building a network before making an offer on a place.

Regarding the timeline of team building, I always stress that developing your network begins on day one. This puts you in the right mindset, in which you—like legendary Bruce Ratner—focus on the people in every project. By the way, Bruce didn't start with a net worth of around $400 million, which he was reported to have after completing more than 50 projects in New York City.[9] In an interview with Crain's New York Business, he shared that he went into the real estate business when he was 38 years old. At the time, he was making $52,000 a year and had two children to support. He thought there might be a better way to improve his income, so he started reaching out to others to learn about opportunities. When building his network, he found a partner and the two started a relationship that spanned more than 30 years. "If it wasn't for them, I would be building walk-ups," he stated. (A "walk-up" refers to an apartment in a residential building that has no elevator; you can only get there by walking up the stairs, thus the name. He was making the point that he wouldn't have found ways to take on big projects, add value, and get outsized returns from his investments.) Instead, by developing a team, he went on to build everything from retail to residential to office to hotel. The returns followed.[10]

Today, Bruce is also known as a philanthropist and has been recognized for his contributions to cancer research.[11] He was behind the creation of the Living Holocaust Memorial at the Auschwitz Jewish Center Foundation at the Museum of Jewish Heritage in New York. Perhaps his charity work, along with his dedication to building a strong team, reflects on the full-circle effect that real estate investments can make. After all, if it begins with people, it also ends with people (and the cycle repeats).

For Bruce, there was an extra, intangible benefit from working on his various projects, no matter how complicated they were. "I never got that much of a thrill from saying, 'I built the tallest this or the most beautiful that,'" he explained in the interview with Crain's New York Business. "It's always been people using the buildings that's excited me. I look at people passing through Metrotech and using the commons, people going to the arena, the way the New York Times uses its building. That, to me, is what is actually important."[12]

KEY TAKEAWAYS

- While a reliable team is essential for lasting success, you can get started in real estate investing when you have as little as one solid connection. A good investment sales broker or attorney can make introductions to other trusted professionals.

- The right team will help you spot opportunities to add value you might have not seen on your own—and they'll help you avoid missteps that could have cost you deeply.

- Looking for ways to give can have a reciprocal positive impact, as others will remember your generosity and may repay you in the future.

- Building your real estate investment network takes time and is an ongoing effort: look for ways to continually meet people, stay connected, and have fun along the way.

FINAL THOUGHTS

As they say in filming, "That's a wrap!" And yet, I truly hope for you it is the beginning of a journey that leads to returns that outperform the market and gives you both the return you're hoping for and a lot of great stories, adventures, and feelings of gratitude along the way.

If you're wondering when to start, my best advice is one word: now. There's no better way to learn than by doing. Take this book and use it as your guide. You will make mistakes along the way (as did I), but that is part of the investing experience. Successful investors evaluate the pitfalls and change course as needed. The learning process is ongoing. I continue to add more insight and takeaways to my career, as I go through the transactions and work with others who are out there, pounding the pavement day after day in their respective areas of expertise.

You might find it helpful to create a timeline for the steps in the process, such as the one displayed in Figure 12.1.

Figure 12.1 A timeline from step 1 to step 10

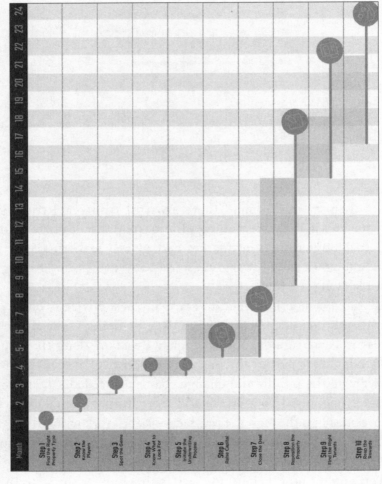

Credit: John Santoro, graphic designer at Avison Young in New York City

There's no need to try to overthink the market. From my experience, those who try to analyze every facet and detail of each trend end up never buying anything. If you start small and put in the parameters we've established so you don't place yourself in financial risk, you'll be able to manage your investments.

Here are five bonus takeaways to inspire you on your journey:

1. **Learn from the best.** Listen to my series of podcasts in which I interview successful investors. They can be found at jamesnelson.com. In these conversations, real estate professionals share everything from how they started to the missteps they made and the joy they get out what they do. You'll see that it's possible to come from any walk of life, provided you have the drive to gather the resources and work with others to get on your way.

2. **Leverage the data.** Today, all the information you need about a property can be found online—you just have to know where to find it. Look for services like PropertyShark or the Automated City Register Information System (ACRIS), or ask others in your area what they use. I did a three-part series on leveraging data on my podcast: look for it at jamesnelson.com/podcast. There are also predictive analysis tools, including Property IDX, which my friend Ash Zandieh is behind. The platform can help determine who likely sellers might be, based on their traditional hold periods and building traits.

3. **Never stop learning.** We are in the information business, so commit to being a voracious reader and listener. Every morning, I read news publications and check social media feeds for sales information. I also listen to podcasts such as *America's Commercial Real Estate Show*, *Bisnow Reports*, *Changing Places*, *Deconstruct*, *Driven by Insight*, *Investing in the U.S.*, *The Massimo Show*, and *Weekly Take*. I have several friends with podcasts, including *Behind the Bricks*, *Big Money*

Energy, Coffee & Cap Rates, Conversations with Cohen, Leasing Reality, Real Tech Talk with Eric Brody, and *Realty Speak.*

4. **Make a name for yourself.** After you have a couple of sales under your belt and a track record, share the news. Promote your sales to the press, post them on social media, start a newsletter that discusses what you see in the market, and so on. These steps will help you become that go-to person that brokers call when they have a great deal on their hands.

5. **Seek out ways to give.** I'm a big proponent of paying it back, as well as paying it forward. Two of my favorite books are Adam Grant's *Give and Take* and *How to Win Friends and Influence People* by Dale Carnegie. Relationships are a two-way street, and you'll go far if you continually offer to help others in return—or better yet, without expecting anything in return.

Finally, I believe in not just talking the talk, but also walking the walk. With that in mind, please look for me on social media and connect. I'm always open to building up networks together, and you can find me at:

My website: jamesnelson.com

LinkedIn: JamesNelsonNYC

Twitter: JamesNelsonNYC

Instagram: @jamesnelsonnyc

Thank you and I wish you nothing but the best for a successful journey filled with game-changing strategies that outperform the market.

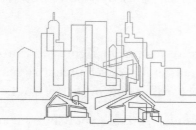

GLOSSARY

Key Real Estate Terms for Investors

30/360: A calculation used to determine the interest rate for a loan. It assumes that every month has 30 days and there are 360 days in a year.

1031 exchange: The act of switching one investment property for another to defer taxes on capital gains.

Absolute NNN lease: A commercial lease in which the tenant is responsible for all expenses related to the building, including maintenance and repairs to the property's structure. In these cases, the tenant virtually owns the property without having the buy it.

Acquisition loans: A loan that is created to allow you to go acquire a property.

Actual/360: A way to calculate the interest rate for a loan that is based on the actual number of days in a month. It assumes there are 360 days in a year.

Air rights: Residual development rights for a property. Also known in some cases as transferable development rights (TDRs). These are subject to zoning regarding how or if they can be used.

Amortization schedule: A table showing the repayment schedule of a loan, typically broken out between interest and principal, and showing the beginning and ending balance of the loan balance after payments are made.

Asset class: The term given to a group of investment products that share common features and behave in a similar way in the market-place. In real estate, the main asset classes are multifamily, retail, office, and land.

Asset manager: Someone who makes investment decisions on behalf of a group of investors or a real estate fund.

Assumable loan: A loan that is transferable to a purchasing party in the conveyance of a property.

Auction: An on-market listing that is usually supported by a listing agent. The sale process can take place in multiple formats, ranging from the courtroom steps to online platforms.

Basis point: A term that describes the differences and changes in interest rates. One basis point is 0.01%, so 100 basis points are 1%.

Bridge loan: A short-term loan that can be used while you secure final financing for a transaction.

Broker: In real estate, a broker is a professional who has the necessary license to act as an intermediary in the selling, purchasing, and renting of real estate. Brokers might carry out orders related to multifamily, retail, office, or land properties. In many cases the term can be used interchangeably with the term "agent." In some states, "broker" refers to the broker of record for a firm which has oversight, whereas sales agents must work under a broker.

Business plan: In real estate, this refers to a document that outlines the strategy related to an investment on a property. It will present goals for the property, milestones for projects carried out, and details on how the objectives will be achieved.

Buyer broker: Occasionally referred to as a buyer's agent, this professional is responsible for representing the interests of an individual or party who wants to purchase a property. The buyer broker receives a fee or commission for their services. The fee may be paid by the buyer or the seller, but all fees need to be disclosed to all parties.

Buyer specific representation: An off-market listing in which a broker will get recognized by the seller to bring a specific buyer.

Cap: The maximum rate that a lender can charge on a loan.

Capital expenditures: Funds used to add on to or improve a property that go beyond regular maintenance.

Capital gains tax: The tax applied to the profits earned from the sale of an asset. In real estate, capital gains taxes may be associated with the sale of property.

Capital stack: The equity and debt used to acquire a property as a real estate investment.

Capitalization rate: The net operating income of an investment property divided by the purchase price.

Cash flow: In real estate, a term that describes the difference between how much income a property generates and its expenses, including loan payments. It is calculated by taking the net operating income less debt service.

Cash-on-cash return: A calculation of the cash flow from the property divided by the amount of equity you have in the investment.

Cash out: The amount you can take out when refinancing and taking out a new loan to cover the property's value.

Commercial Mortgage-Backed Securities: Often referred to as CMBS, this is a loan option for real estate investors who want to purchase income-producing properties. These loans often have more flexible terms and underwriting requirements than other types of loans issued by banks and financial institutions.

Closing: The last stage of the loan process when purchasing property, in which the title of the property passes from the seller to the buyer.

Concession: A compromise between a tenant and owner or landlord in which the owner or landlord typically offers an incentive for the tenant to sign the lease.

Construction loan: A loan that is usually issued by a bank to carry out construction.

Credit tenant: Institutional-grade tenants who are rated. Agencies such as Moody's will rate the strength of their credit. A credit tenant has exceptionally high credit. The client typically is substantial in size and considered to be stable, such as a major corporation.

Debt-to-income ratio: The amount you owe each month divided by your monthly income.

Debt service: The amount of cash needed to pay for the interest, principal, and any other fees related to a debt for a period.

Debt service coverage ratio: The net operating income from a property divided by the annual debt service.

Debt yield: The net operating income from a property divided by the loan amount.

Due diligence: In real estate, the term refers to steps that a person or company carries out to investigate a property. It consists of a review of the property's financial records, including a lease and tenant review. It also includes an evaluation of the property condition and environmental reports.

Effective gross income: The gross revenue minus the vacancy and credit loss.

Encumbrance: A claim against a property by a party other than the owner.

Escrow: A legal arrangement in which a third party holds money or property until a condition is met. In real estate, funds from the sale of a property might be held in escrow until the next purchase agreement is signed.

Estoppel certificate: An agreement that describes the current conditions of a lease. It includes details about the relationship between the tenants and landlord, and information about the rent and when it is due.

Exclusive agency: An on-market listing in which the seller has a broker. However, the seller has the ability to sell the property directly to their own buyers without having to compensate the listing broker. The broker is only compensated if they bring the ultimate buyer.

Exclusive right to sell: An on-market listing in which the seller has engaged a sales broker to run a full marketing process.

Fair market value: The price for which a property will sell or rent, based on the surrounding market conditions.

Finder's fee: In real estate, an amount paid to a person or firm for bringing an opportunity to investors.

Fixed expenses: In real estate, costs that don't readily change, including real estate taxes and insurance premiums. They may be adjusted on an annual basis.

Fixed rate: An interest rate that will not change during the term of the loan.

Floating rate: An interest rate attached to a loan that can fluctuate; the rate typically changes at set intervals, such as once a month.

For sale by owner (FSBO): An off-market listing in which an owner looks to sell the property on their own.

Full-service lease: Also called a gross lease, under this arrangement the tenant pays a base rent. The landlord covers additional building expenses, such as maintenance fees, insurance, and real estate taxes.

Grandfathering: In real estate, the term refers to a building that does not have to follow a current zoning or building code because it was legally operating before the code came into effect.

Gross domestic product: Often referred to as GDP, this metric measures the value of goods and services produced in an area during a set period.

Gross potential rent revenue: An amount that depicts the most rental income that can be generated from a property.

Gross revenue: In real estate, the term refers to the total proceeds related to a property, which could include rents from residential and commercial tenants. If tenants pay toward operating expenses, this amount is frequently included in the gross revenue too.

Income statement: A document that lists the revenue and expenses from a property over a period, to show how the investment performed. The income statement is sometimes referred to as the pro forma, P&L (profit and loss), or a broker setup.

Industrial leasing broker: An intermediary involved in finding and negotiating with companies interested in warehousing space, production facilities, or other industrial properties.

Institutional investors: Companies or organizations with employees who invest on behalf of others, such as other companies or organizations.

Interest-only (IO): A debt service payment in which the entire amount of the payment consists of interest expense. No portion of payment goes to reduce the principal balance of the loan.

Internal rate of return (IRR): The internal rate of return over the life of the investment. The IRR determines the investment's overall profitability by calculating the net present value (NPV) of the future cashflows, including refinances or the ultimate sale.

Investment sales broker: A broker who represents investors in the buying and selling of properties. An investment sales broker typically charges a fee or commission for executing buy and sell orders.

Joint venture agreement: A business arrangement in which two or more partners combine their resources for a real estate investment; it dictates how the profits will be distributed among the parties involved.

Landlord-tenant attorney: An attorney who specializes in the laws surrounding the rights of tenants and landlords.

Land use attorney: An attorney who reviews legal issues related to the development of a property. The land use attorney will advise according to zoning laws, construction permits, and other legal matters related to the project.

Lease guarantee: An agreement signed by the landlord, tenant, and a third party who meets the financial requirements established by the landlord. The third party agrees to be a guarantor and assumes responsibility for a default in rent.

Leasing broker: Sometimes referred to as a landlord broker or an agency broker, this professional represents the owner or landlord in a real estate transaction. The leasing broker may market the property, coordinate the showing to prospective tenants, help advise both tenants and landlords during the leasing process, and arrange the lease signing of a property with tenants. The individual receives a fee or commission for their services.

Leasing commission: A fee that is paid to a leasing agent for bringing in a tenant. It is usually a percentage-based charge.

Letter of intent: An agreement that lists the terms of the sale. It is used as a draft agreement, on which the finalized contract is based. The letter of intent can be nonbinding, or it can be a binding document that will grant exclusivity but will be finalized by a purchase and sale agreement.

Leverage: The use of borrowed capital or debt to increase the return on an investment.

Lien: A legal right or claim that a creditor has over a property; they are often associated with collateral in loans.

Like-kind properties: Properties that are of the same nature or character. They could differ in grade or quality.

Listing: An agreement that names someone else, typically a broker or real estate agent, to handle the sale of a property and receive a fee or a commission for their services.

Loan agreement: A binding contract between the lender and another party (or parties) to formalize a loan process.

Loan to cost: The amount of the loan divided by the total project cost.

Loan to purchase price: The loan amount divided by the price the buyer is paying for the property.

Loan to value: The loan amount divided by the total value of the property.

London Interbank Offer Rate (LIBOR): The old benchmark interest rate that major global banks used to lend funds to each other. It is being replaced by the Secured Overnight Financing Rate (SOFR).

Managing agent: Also known as a property manager or third-party manager, this person or company is hired by a property owner or landlord to oversee the day-to-day requirements of the building. Their responsibilities include collecting rents, creating financial reports, overseeing maintenance and repair work, and maintaining communication with the tenants. They also enforce the rules related to a property, along with the terms of the leases and the lease extensions.

Metropolitan Statistical Area: An urbanized area with a population of at least 50,000, according to the US Office of Management and Budget. It's the formal definition of a region that has a city and surrounding communities that are linked by social and economic factors. They are used to show which geographic areas have high population densities.

Mezzanine debt: A nontraditional form of financing that mixes debt with equity. In the capital stack, it has higher risk than senior debt and lower risk than preferred equity and common equity. It also has greater rewards than senior debt, but fewer than preferred equity and common equity.

Modified gross lease: A commercial lease that is in between the full-service lease and a triple net lease. It usually means that the tenant pays base rent, utilities, and part of the operating costs for the property.

Mortgage: A loan used to purchase a type of real estate, such as a home or land.

Mortgage broker: An intermediary who brings together mortgage lenders with mortgage borrowers but does not originate or service the loans. A mortgage broker receives a fee for facilitating the transactions between lenders and borrowers.

Net lease: A lease in which the tenant pays a portion of the building's operating expenses. They might help cover maintenance in common areas, property taxes, and insurance. There are three types of net leases: single, double, and triple. For a single net lease, the tenant pays for rent and utilities plus property taxes; with a double net lease, the tenant pays for rent and utilities plus property taxes and building insurance; and under a triple net lease, the tenant pays for rent and utilities plus property taxes, building insurance, and all other operating expenses.

Net operating income: In real estate, a calculation that shows total revenue from a property, minus all the operating expenses.

Note: A promise to pay back a loan.

Office leasing broker: An intermediary who helps negotiate terms with tenants in workspaces.

Operating expenses: All the costs associated with running a property, including real estate taxes, insurance, heat, water and sewer, and repairs and maintenance.

Overleverage: To carry too much debt; to borrow to the extent that the borrower is unable to make interest payments, principal payments, or cover operating expenses due to the heavy debt burden.

Owner-occupied property: A multifamily property in which the owner lives in one of the units. This term can also apply to commercial users, such as a company purchasing an office building for their own use.

Owner's representative: An individual who looks out for the owner's interests and goals on a project.

Pass-through expense: A cost related to a property that the occupying tenant pays. The expense passes from the landlord to the tenant.

Percentage lease: A commercial lease in which the tenant pays a base rent along with a percentage of the gross business sales. This percentage is typically paid once a certain threshold has been met.

Permanent loan: A loan on a property that generally has a fixed interest rate and a term that lasts between 10 and 30 years.

Preemptive offer: A bid placed on a property before the seller's designated date to consider offers.

Preferred equity: In real estate, investors contribute money to a project and agree to a set return on their investment. In the capital stack, this has greater risk than mezzanine debt and senior debt, and lower risk than common equity. Its reward potential is higher than mezzanine debt and senior debt but below that attached to common equity.

Prepayment penalties: Additional fees the borrower will be charged if the loan is repaid before its maturity date.

Price per square foot (PPSF): A term used to describe the value of a property. It is calculated by dividing the price of the building by the number of square feet.

Primary market: Large metropolitan areas with high population densities, robust economies, and job opportunities. In the United States, New York City is the #1 primary market, followed by Los Angeles, Chicago, and San Francisco.

Pro rata: A method of calculating the expenses for which the seller will resume responsibility, and those that the buyer will cover, in order to close on a property.

Promote: A term referring to the share of profits a sponsor receives from a real estate investment once a certain threshold for the return is reached.

Property disclosure statement: Documentation that outlines any flaws related to a property that could negatively affect its value.

Property manager: Also known as a managing agent or third-party manager, this person or company is hired by a property owner or landlord to oversee the day-to-day requirements of the building. Their responsibilities include collecting rents, creating financial reports, overseeing maintenance and repair work, and maintaining communication with the tenants. They also enforce the rules related to a property, along with the terms of the leases and the lease extensions.

Punch list: A document that is often created toward the end of a construction project. It lists the repairs, fixes, and minor tasks that need to be finished or resolved for the project to be considered complete.

Purchase and sale agreement (PSA): A legally binding document that addresses the purchase price of a property and the financing to pay for it. It also outlines the deposit amount, information about the sale, and conditions that would warrant the contract to be terminated.

Real estate fund: An entity that is formed to pool money from a group of investors. The fund is then used to purchase, hold, manage, and sell properties on behalf of the investors. Those who contribute receive a return based on the terms outlined in an agreement.

Retail leasing broker: An intermediary who assists with the process of renting out retail properties.

Rent regulation: Sometimes referred to as rent control, this government policy limits the amount a landlord can charge when leasing a property or renewing a lease. The laws for rent regulation differ from one city to the next, as they are usually governed at the municipality level. The goal of rent regulation is to keep the cost of living at an affordable rate for low-income households.

Rent roll: A document that lists out rents that are due and rents that have been collected on a property with tenants. A rent roll will include the gross, or total, rent collected. It makes it easy to see the income stream from the place, though it may not include expenses such as a mortgage payment, insurance, taxes, or utilities.

Return on investment: In real estate, this refers to the net operating income divided by the sum of the purchase price, renovation costs, and leasing costs.

SEC: The US Securities and Exchange Commission, a US government agency which oversees the protection of investors and enforces laws against market manipulation.

Secondary market: An up-and-coming market, with rent and housing prices that are on the rise and a fluctuation of workers moving in.

Secured Overnight Financing Rate (SOFR): A rate that is based on the overnight interest rates for loans and derivatives in US dollars. SOFR is replacing LIBOR as the benchmark interest rate.

Selling broker: Occasionally called a seller's agent, this professional is responsible for representing the interests of an individual or party who wants to sell a property. The selling broker receives a fee or commission for their services.

Senior debt: The mortgage lender or debt holder who has the highest claim on a property. In the capital stack, senior debt has the position with the least amount of risk and also the lowest reward. If the borrower is unable to pay the mortgage, the senior debt institution will take over the property and resell it to cover their losses.

Sources and uses: A document that shows the capital stack and how the funds will be used in the acquisition of a property.

Spread: The premium that the lender receives for making a loan. It is a certain amount above an index and is often expressed in basis points.

Swap: An exchange of interest rates, such as a switch from a floating interest rate to a fixed rate, or vice versa.

Sweat equity: In real estate investments, a nonmonetary contribution that consists of time and labor.

Tax attorney: A finance professional who specializes in tax policies and offers guidance to clients on tax-related matters.

Tax lien: A legal claim against a property for tax bills that are owed and haven't been paid.

Tertiary market: Cities and towns that fall below primary and secondary markets. They are typically not as well-known as large metropolitan areas and have a population of 1 million or less. The rent and home prices are generally lower than those found in primary and secondary markets.

Third-party manager: A person or company that oversees the responsibilities related to an asset; in real estate, a third-party manager may also be known as a managing agent or property manager. This person or company is hired by a property owner or landlord to oversee the day-to-day requirements of the building. Their responsibilities include collecting rents, creating financial reports, overseeing maintenance and repair work, and maintaining communication with the tenants. They also enforce the rules related to a property, along with the terms of the leases and the lease extensions.

Title agent: A professional who is responsible for verifying that a title on a piece of real estate is valid; they typically issue title insurance to buyers.

Title insurance: A policy that protects buyers from financial loss or legal expenses that stem from defects in the property's title.

Title search: An examination of the public records to determine and confirm a property's legal ownership. If there are any claims or liens on the property, they should be revealed during this initial investigation.

Time of Essence: Often stated as TOE, a "time is of the essence" clause in a contract means the buyer must close by a certain date, regardless of whether financing was obtained. If the closing doesn't take place within the given time, the buyer is in breach of contract; the down payment and building are lost.

Total project cost: The amount needed for a real estate project, including acquisition costs, closing costs, hard costs, and soft costs.

Transactional real estate attorney: A professional who works to ensure the legal transfer of a property during a sale. During the transaction that shifts the property from the seller to the buyer, the transactional real estate attorney will be involved in the contracts, loan documents, title documents, and other legal work related to the sale. They will also be present during the closing.

Underwriting: In real estate investing, an evaluation of the property's cash flow, rate of return of the investment, and the borrower's ability to pay back any loans taken out related to the purchase. Through the underwriting process, lenders take on financial risk in exchange for a fee.

Upzone: To change the zoning codes to allow for a higher or more dense building.

Vacancy and credit loss: The estimated amount of rental income that is lost, due to vacant units or nonpayments of rent.

Variable expenses: In real estate, costs that can increase or decrease depending on factors such as number of units paying rent. These might include heat, water and sewer, and repairs and maintenance.

Walk-up: An apartment in a residential building that has no elevator; it is only accessible by walking up a staircase, which is usually located outside the building.

Waterfall: A predetermined structure or model in real estate investing that shows how the cash will flow to different investors based on their agreement and level of participation in an investment.

Well-capitalized: Having enough financial resources to operate without severe monetary constraint. In real estate, this often means having a group of investors, along with financing, to carry out an investment.

Yield: The income returned on an investment.

Zoning: The municipal or local laws and regulations that direct how property can or cannot be used in a certain geographic area.

NOTES

PROLOGUE

1. "Mark Twain Quotes." Brainy Quote. https://www.brainyquote.com /quotes/mark_twain_380355. Last accessed May 3, 2022.
2. "Massey Knakal Realty Services." The Real Deal. https://therealdeal .com/new-research/topics/company/massey-knakal-realty-services/#:~: text=Massey%20Knakal%20Realty%20Services%20was,2014%20for %20approximately%20%24100%20million. Accessed May 3, 2022.

INTRODUCTION

1. "Estimating the Size of the Commercial Real Estate Market in the U.S." Nareit. https://www.reit.com/data-research/research/nareit-research /estimating-size-commercial-real-estate-market-us-2021. Last accessed March 13, 2022.

STEP 1

1. "Mobile Home Park Investing – A Superior Asset Class." SMK Capital Management. https://smkcap.com/mobile-home-park-investing -a-superior-asset-class/.
2. "Zell Reflects on His Decades-Long Career." Pollack, Lynn. Globe St. April 28, 2021. https://www.globest.com/2021/04/28/sam-zell-reflects -on-his-decades-long-career/?slreturn=20220211112138.

3. Sam Zell. *Am I Being Too Subtle? Straight Talk From a Business Rebel.* Portfolio, 2017.

4. "Zell Reflects on His Decades-Long Career." Pollack, Lynn. Globe St. April 28, 2021. https://www.globest.com/2021/04/28/sam-zell-reflects -on-his-decades-long-career/?slreturn=20220211112138.

5. "How Sam Zell Made His Fortune." Investopedia. Cassell, Warren Jr. October 7, 2020. https://www.investopedia.com/articles/investing /102915/how-sam-zell-made-his-fortune.asp.

6. Pollack, Lynn. "Multi-family Is CRE's Most Liquid Sector." Globe St. June 7, 2021. https://www.globest.com/2021/06/07/multifamily-is-cres -most-liquid-sector/.

7. "2022 Trends and Trade Report Data." Real Capital Analytics. https:// www.msci.com/our-solutions/real-assets/real-capital-analytics.

8. Namaste, Justice. "How WeWork Rebounded After its Controversial IPO." March 18, 2022. Bustle.com. https://www.bustle.com /entertainment/does-wework-still-exist-who-owns-it-now.

STEP 2

1. "How Bruce Ratner Became One of New York City's Top Developers." October 29, 2019. *The Insider's Edge to Real Estate Investing* podcast. https://jamesnelson.com/podcast.

2. "Bruce Ratner." TRD Topics, TRData. The Real Deal. https:// therealdeal.com/new-research/topics/people/bruce-ratner/. Last accessed April 4, 2022.

STEP 4

1. Gordon, Lisa Kaplan. "What Are Property Disclosure Statements? Info Buyers Need to Know." March 4, 2022. Realtor.com. https://www .realtor.com/advice/buy/what-is-a-property-disclosure-statement/.

2. "Phase 2 Environmental Assessment Sample Clauses." *Law Insider*. https://www.lawinsider.com/clause/phase-ii-environmental-assessment. Last accessed June 13, 2022.

3. Rahman, Pinaaz. "Difference Between Phase 1, Phase 2, and Phase 3 Environmental Site Inspection." June 1, 2020. Pryco Global. https:// prycoglobal.com/blog/difference-between-phase-i-phase-ii-phase-iii -esa/.

4. "How to Identify Replacement Property." Legal 1031 Exchange Services, LLC. https://legal1031.com/1031-exchange-resources/how-to-identify-replacement-property/. Last accessed April 8, 2022.
5. "New York City Zoning Handbook." 2018 Edition. New York City Department of Planning. https://www1.nyc.gov/site/planning/zoning/zh.page.
6. "Greenwich Village History." Learn Village History. https://www.villagepreservation.org/resources/neighborhood-history/#nineteenth-century. Last accessed April 7, 2022.
7. "From Multi-Family to Student Housing with Margaret Streicker." January 28, 2020. *The Insider's Edge to Real Estate Investing* podcast. https://jamesnelson.com/podcast
8. "TRD Topics: Margaret Streicker Porres." The Real Deal. https://therealdeal.com/new-research/topics/people/margaret-streicker-porres/. Last accessed April 7, 2022.

STEP 5

1. "Building Passive Income: An Interview with Doug Marshall." November 19, 2019. *The Insider's Edge to Real Estate Investing* podcast. https://jamesnelson.com/podcast
2. Sachs, Ian. "The History of Insurance Underwriting Explained in 2 Minutes." August 17, 2021. LinkedIn. https://www.linkedin.com/pulse/history-insurance-underwriting-explained-2-minutes-sachs-cfp-clu-/.
3. Rathburn, Pete. "What Is Underwriting?" August 18, 2021. Investopedia. https://www.investopedia.com/ask/answers/100214/what-real-estate-underwriting.asp.
4. "Building Passive Income: An Interview with Doug Marshall." November 19, 2019. *The Insider's Edge to Real Estate Investing* podcast. https://jamesnelson.com/podcast.
5. "Building Passive Income: An Interview with Doug Marshall." November 19, 2019. *The Insider's Edge to Real Estate Investing* podcast. https://jamesnelson.com/podcast.
6. "Building Passive Income: An Interview with Doug Marshall." November 19, 2019. *The Insider's Edge to Real Estate Investing* podcast. https://jamesnelson.com/podcast.
7. "Building Passive Income: An Interview with Doug Marshall." November 19, 2019. *The Insider's Edge to Real Estate Investing* podcast. https://jamesnelson.com/podcast.

8. "Building Passive Income: An Interview with Doug Marshall." November 19, 2019. *The Insider's Edge to Real Estate Investing* podcast. https://jamesnelson.com/podcast.

STEP 6

1. "Jordan Vogel: Says Just Do It." James Nelson podcast. January 14, 2020. www.jamesnelson.com/podcast.
2. "Jordan Vogel interview." Marcus & Millichap NYM Group. https://newyorkmultifamily.com/jordan-vogel-interview/#:~:text=Jordan%20Vogel%20is%20the%20co,New%20York%20City%20apartment%20buildings. Last accessed May 5, 2022.
3. "Benchmark Real Estate Group." https://benchmarkrealestate.com/. Last accessed May 6, 2022.
4. Kirshenbaum, Warren. "Taking Credit: Historic Preservation Tax Incentives Offer Capital Solutions." CIRE Magazine. https://www.ccim.com/cire-magazine/articles/287296/2013/03/taking-credit/.
5. "What Are Historic Tax Credits?" Commercial Real Estate Loans. https://www.commercialrealestate.loans/commercial-real-estate-glossary/historic-tax-credits-htc. Last accessed May 12, 2022.
6. "What Are Historic Tax Credits?" Commercial Real Estate Loans. https://www.commercialrealestate.loans/commercial-real-estate-glossary/historic-tax-credits-htc. Last accessed May 12, 2022.

STEP 7

1. "Leading by Example: MaryAnne Gilmartin Re-Broadcast." December 3, 2021. *The Insider's Edge to Real Estate Investing* podcast. https://jamesnelson.com/podcast.
2. Birch, Dr. Eugenie, Amanda Lloyd, MCP. "Case Study: Atlantic Yards, Brooklyn New York." September 15, 2020. Wilson Center. https://penniur.upenn.edu/uploads/media/Atlantic_Yards_Case_Study_September_2020.pdf.
3. Rittie, Jason. "Caveat Emptor: 'Let the Buyer Beware' – Due Diligence in Commercial Real Estate Purchases." February 25, 2020. Einhorn Barbarito Attorneys at Law. https://www.einhornlawyers.com/blog/real-estate/caveat-emptor-let-buyer-beware-due-diligence-commercial-real-estate-purchases/.

4. Rittie, Jason. "Caveat Emptor: 'Let the Buyer Beware' – Due Diligence in Commercial Real Estate Purchases." February 25, 2020. Einhorn Barbarito Attorneys at Law. https://www.einhornlawyers.com/blog/real -estate/caveat-emptor-let-buyer-beware-due-diligence-commercial-real -estate-purchases/.

5. Frank, Jeri. "How to do a Property Title Search for Your Commercial Property." October 1, 2020. Stratafolio. https://stratafolio.com/how-to -do-a-property-title-search-for-your-commercial-property/.

6. Rittie, Jason. "Caveat Emptor: 'Let the Buyer Beware' – Due Diligence in Commercial Real Estate Purchases." February 25, 2020. Einhorn Barbarito Attorneys at Law. https://www.einhornlawyers.com/blog/real -estate/caveat-emptor-let-buyer-beware-due-diligence-commercial-real -estate-purchases/.

7. Cauble, Tyler. "Step by Step: Commercial Real Estate Due Diligence." December 22, 2020. The Cauble Group. https://www.tylercauble.com /blog/commercia-real-estate-due-diligence.

8. Cauble, Tyler. "Step by Step: Commercial Real Estate Due Diligence." December 22, 2020. The Cauble Group. https://www.tylercauble.com /blog/commercia-real-estate-due-diligence.

9. "What is Environmental Due Diligence? A Complete Guide." September 1, 2020. Millman Blog. https://millmanland.com/industry -news/what-is-environmental-due-diligence/.

10. Rohde, Jeff. "What is Due Diligence in Real Estate?" October 2, 2021. Roofstock. https://learn.roofstock.com/blog/what-is-due-diligence-in -real-estate.

11. "Lessons Learned from a Conversation with Jeff Ravetz." December 10, 2019. *The Insider's Edge to Real Estate Investing* podcast. https:// jamesnelson.com/podcast.

12. Ganti, Akhilesh. "Metropolitan Statistical Area (MSA)." October 31, 2021. Investopedia. https://www.investopedia.com/terms/m/msa.asp.

13. Rohde, Jeff. "Understanding Primary vs. Secondary Markets in Real Estate." December 7, 2021. Roofstock. https://learn.roofstock.com/blog /primary-vs-secondary-markets-real-estate.

14. Rohde, Jeff. "Understanding Primary vs. Secondary Markets in Real Estate." December 7, 2021. Roofstock. https://learn.roofstock.com/blog /primary-vs-secondary-markets-real-estate.

15. Rohde, Jeff. "Understanding Primary vs. Secondary Markets in Real Estate." December 7, 2021. Roofstock. https://learn.roofstock.com/blog /primary-vs-secondary-markets-real-estate.

16. Rohde, Jeff. "What Are Tertiary Markets in Real Estate?" August 20, 2021. https://learn.roofstock.com/blog/tertiary-market-real-estate.

17. Cauble, Tyler. "Step by Step: Commercial Real Estate Due Diligence." December 22, 2020. The Cauble Group. https://www.tylercauble.com /blog/commercia-real-estate-due-diligence

STEP 8

1. "Lessons Learned from a Conversation with Jeff Ravetz." December 10, 2019. *The Insider's Edge to Real Estate Investing* podcast. https://jamesnelson.com/podcast.

2. "Lessons Learned from a Conversation with Jeff Ravetz." December 10, 2019. *The Insider's Edge to Real Estate Investing* podcast. https://jamesnelson.com/podcast.

3. "Lessons Learned from a Conversation with Jeff Ravetz." December 10, 2019. *The Insider's Edge to Real Estate Investing* podcast. https://jamesnelson.com/podcast.

4. "Lessons Learned from a Conversation with Jeff Ravetz." December 10, 2019. *The Insider's Edge to Real Estate Investing* podcast. https://jamesnelson.com/podcast.

5. "Lessons Learned from a Conversation with Jeff Ravetz." December 10, 2019. *The Insider's Edge to Real Estate Investing* podcast. https://jamesnelson.com/podcast.

6. "Lessons Learned from a Conversation with Jeff Ravetz." December 10, 2019. *The Insider's Edge to Real Estate Investing* podcast. https://jamesnelson.com/podcast.

7. "Lessons Learned from a Conversation with Jeff Ravetz." December 10, 2019. *The Insider's Edge to Real Estate Investing* podcast. https://jamesnelson.com/podcast.

8. "Lessons Learned from a Conversation with Jeff Ravetz." December 10, 2019. *The Insider's Edge to Real Estate Investing* podcast. https://jamesnelson.com/podcast.

9. "Lessons Learned from a Conversation with Jeff Ravetz." December 10, 2019. *The Insider's Edge to Real Estate Investing* podcast. https://jamesnelson.com/podcast.

STEP 9

1. "No Experience Required with Chad Cooley." February 4, 2020. *The Insider's Edge to Real Estate Investing* podcast. https://jamesnelson.com /podcast.
2. "No Experience Required with Chad Cooley." February 4, 2020. *The Insider's Edge to Real Estate Investing* podcast. https://jamesnelson.com /podcast.
3. "No Experience Required with Chad Cooley." February 4, 2020. *The Insider's Edge to Real Estate Investing* podcast. https://jamesnelson.com /podcast.
4. "No Experience Required with Chad Cooley." February 4, 2020. *The Insider's Edge to Real Estate Investing* podcast. https://jamesnelson.com /podcast.
5. "No Experience Required with Chad Cooley." February 4, 2020. *The Insider's Edge to Real Estate Investing* podcast. https://jamesnelson.com /podcast.
6. Turner, Brandon. "The Landlord's Guide to Rental Property Security Deposits." September, 2020. BiggerPockets.com. https://www .biggerpockets.com/blog/rental-property-security-deposits.
7. Olsen, Eirik. "Everything You Need to Know About Non-Refundable Deposits—Bellevue Property Management." April 21, 2015. SJA Property Management. https://propertymanagersseattle .com/everything-you-need-to-know-about-non-refundable-deposits -bellevue-property-management/.
8. Taylor, McHargue. "What Is a Lease Guarantee?" Aquila Commercial. https://aquilacommercial.com/learning-center/what-is-a-lease -guarantee/#:~:text=A%20lease%20guarantee%20is%20an,protects %20the%20tenant%20from%20eviction. Last accessed May 13, 2022.
9. "What Is a Lease Agreement Good-Guy Guarantee?" Franchise Law Solutions. https://www.franchiselawsolutions.com/lease-reviews/good -guy-guarantee/#:~:text=If%20you're%20a%20tenant,a%20lease%20is %20terminated%20early. Last accessed May 13, 2022.
10. "How Much Rent Can I Afford?" Renthop. https://www.renthop.com /rent-calculator. Last accessed May 13, 2022.
11. "How Much Rent Can I Afford?" Renthop. https://www.renthop.com /rent-calculator. Last accessed May 13, 2022.

12. McGarvey, Cassandra. "Commercial Landlords: Do Your Due Diligence." February 5, 2021. McGarvey PLLC. https://www .mcgarveypllc.com/commercial-landlords-do-your-due-diligence/.

STEP 10

1. "Risk Game with Francis Greenburger." May 26, 2020. *The Insider's Edge to Real Estate Investing* podcast. https://jamesnelson.com/podcast.

2. Risk Game with Francis Greenburger." May 26, 2020. *The Insider's Edge to Real Estate Investing* podcast. https://jamesnelson.com/podcast.

3. Risk Game with Francis Greenburger." May 26, 2020. *The Insider's Edge to Real Estate Investing* podcast. https://jamesnelson.com/podcast.

4. Risk Game with Francis Greenburger." May 26, 2020. *The Insider's Edge to Real Estate Investing* podcast. https://jamesnelson.com/podcast.

5. Royal, James. "What Is the Long-Term Capital Gains Tax?" April 7, 2022. Bankrate.com. https://www.bankrate.com/investing/long-term -capital-gains-tax/#:~:text=Long%2Dterm%20capital%20gains%20tax %20rates%20for%20the%202022%20tax%20year&text=In%202022 %2C%20individual%20filers%20won,rate%20climbs%20to%2020 %20percent.

6. Parys, Sabrina and Tina Orem. April 12, 2022. "2021–2022 Federal Tax Brackets and Federal Income Rates." Nerdwallet.com. https://www .nerdwallet.com/article/taxes/federal-income-tax-brackets.

7. Royal, James. "What Is the Long-Term Capital Gains Tax?" April 7, 2022. Bankrate.com. https://www.bankrate.com/investing/long-term -capital-gains-tax/#:~:text=Long%2Dterm%20capital%20gains%20tax %20rates%20for%20the%202022%20tax%20year&text=In%202022 %2C%20individual%20filers%20won,rate%20climbs%20to%2020 %20percent.

STEP 11

1. "Affirmative Development with Don Peebles." July 7, 2020. *The Insider's Edge to Real Estate Investing* podcast. https://jamesnelson.com/podcast.

2. "The Company." Peebles Corporation. https://peeblescorp.com/about. Last accessed September 24, 2022.

3. "New York Population." PopulationU.com. https://www.populationu .com/us/new-york-population. Last accessed April 6, 2022.

4. "Buildings." The Official Website of The City of New York. https://www1.nyc.gov/assets/sirr/downloads/pdf/Ch4_Buildings_FINAL_singles.pdf

5. Meshel, Jeffrey W. *One Phone Call Away: Secrets of a Master Networker.* Portfolio Hardcover, 2005.

6. "Lessons Learned from a Conversation with Jeff Ravetz." December 10, 2019. *The Insider's Edge to Real Estate Investing* podcast. https://jamesnelson.com/podcast.

7. "Trading Up with Robert Rivani." March 16, 2022. *The Insider's Edge to Real Estate Investing* podcast. https://jamesnelson.com/podcast.

8. "Sourcing with David Shorenstein." March 22, 2022. *The Insider's Edge to Real Estate Investing* podcast. https://jamesnelson.com/podcast.

9. "Bruce Ratner Net Worth." Celebrity Net Worth. https://www.celebritynetworth.com/richest-businessmen/ceos/bruce-ratner-net-worth/. Last accessed April 5, 2022.

10. Geiger, Daniel. "2016 Hall of Fame: Bruce Ratner." *Crain's New York Business.* https://www.crainsnewyork.com/awards/bruce-ratner.

11. "Genentech CEO Bill Anderson and Philanthropist Bruce Ratner to Receive the Cancer Research Institute 2017 Oliver R. Grace Award for Distinguished Service in Advancing Cancer Research." October 10, 2017. Cancer Research Institute. https://www.cancerresearch.org/en-us/news/2017/genentech-bruce-ratner-2017-oliver-r-grace-award.

12. Geiger, Daniel. "2016 Hall of Fame: Bruce Ratner." *Crain's New York Business.* https://www.crainsnewyork.com/awards/bruce-ratner.

INDEX

ABOUT THE AUTHOR

Highly acclaimed investment sales broker James Nelson is principal and head of Avison Young's Tri-State Investment Sales group in New York City. During his 20-plus year career, Nelson has sold more than 500 properties and loans totaling over $5 billion. His accolades include being named Commercial Observer's Power 100, CoStar's Power Broker, and receiving the Deal of the Year award by Real Estate Board of New York.

Nelson is also a serial real estate investor and has launched two real estate funds with total capitalizations of over $350 million. He is passionate about helping others achieve real estate success and offers regular training through his podcast, *The Insider's Edge to Real Estate Investing*. He regularly lectures at Columbia, Fordham, NYU, Wharton, and his alma mater, Colgate. He provides ongoing videos and resources at www.jamesnelson.com.

Nelson's greatest joy stems from spending time with his wife, Allison, and their three sons.